MARRIAGE
A-LA-MODE

D1362171

NEW MERMAIDS

General editors

William C. Carroll, Boston University
Brian Gibbons, University of Münster
Tiffany Stern, University of Oxford

The interior of a Restoration Theatre
drawn by C. Walter Hodges

NEW MERMAIDS

NEW MERMAIDS

JOHN DRYDEN

MARRIAGE A-LA-MODE

edited by David Crane

Methuen Drama • London

New Mermaids

3 5 7 9 10 8 6 4 2

First published 1991
Reprinted with new cover 2002, 2010

Methuen Drama
A & C Black Publishers Limited
36 Soho Square
London W1D 3QY
www.methuendrama.com

ISBN 978 0 7136 6666 3

Copyright © 1991 A & C Black Publishers Limited

Printed in Great Britian by
CPI Bookmarque, Croydon, CR0 4TD

A CIP catalogue record for this book is available
from the British Library

CONTENTS

ACKNOWLEDGEMENTS

I have frequently consulted the standard modern edition of *Marriage A-la-Mode* in volume 11 of the California *Works of John Dryden*, and am greatly indebted to it. I would also like to thank the librarian of the Huntington Library for photocopied material without which the textual work for this edition could not have been completed.

DAVID CRANE

INTRODUCTION

THE AUTHOR

WHAT IS KNOWN about the life of John Dryden almost coincides with what is known about his career as a writer: dramatist, poet, critic, translator, apologist, satirist. That career itself touches upon the social and political life of the second half of the seventeenth century at almost every significant point. It is fair, then, to think of Dryden as a public voice, to think of him as acquiring steadily through the years a position of authority as England's leading man of letters, and to contrast this rise to eminence with the sudden brilliance or fitful performance of writers driven chiefly by private motives and energies.

Dryden began a long way from the London of the royalist Restoration where he spent his life. He was born the eldest son of Erasmus Dryden and his wife, Mary, in August 1631 at Aldwinkle All Saints in Northamptonshire. The family on both sides were staunch puritans. Dryden loved the country and the estate he inherited from his father near Canon's Ashby, and often returned there (he was often enough among friends or family in the country to make it quite possible that the scene at III. i. 137–45 had its roots in his own experience); but he turned decisively away from the religious tradition of his boyhood and was a conventional Anglican and a royalist at the Restoration. By this point, he had been a King's Scholar at Westminster School (1646–50) under the monstrous flogging headmaster, Richard Busby, and pensioner at Trinity College, Cambridge (1650–4) under what must have been a considerably milder regime. Dryden always treated Busby with respect, and he later sent his own sons to Westminster where the old tyrant still presided. It seems significant of a certain strain of insensitivity in him that he respected power even in the hands of an autocrat who must have been responsible during a long life for inflicting much more than the usual share of human misery; and it is perhaps not fanciful to derive the deep, instinctive respect for kingship in *Marriage A-la-Mode* from Dryden's early familiarity with the consequences of pleasing or displeasing a king.

He pleased Busby, and he began early to please King Charles. In 1660 he wrote his poem on the glorious Restoration, *Astraea Redux;* he was elected one of the original Fellows of the Royal Society in November 1662; in 1667 the long poem *Annus Mirabilis* celebrated the English victory against the Dutch; and in 1668 he became poet laureate. The title page of *Marriage A-la-Mode* records the fact of Dryden's status as 'Servant to His Majesty' and the Dedication to Rochester mentions that the king liked this play, as he had liked other of Dryden's work. When *Marriage A-la-Mode* appeared, Dryden's prospects were very bright, and perhaps the name of Henry Herringman at the foot of the title page reminded him of the small beginnings of his serious literary career with a commission from the same bookseller three years before the return of the king.

Dryden wrote reluctantly for the theatre, if we are to believe his own account, and even more reluctantly wrote comedy (see Dedication 17), but it was the theatre that gave him financial security to match his rising literary reputation. He had married Lady Elizabeth Howard in 1663 and by 1669 had three sons, so a good income was essential. After *Marriage A-la-Mode*, however, which is generally considered his finest comedy, and *All for Love* (1677), his greatest tragedy and the only play, as Dryden says, that he wrote for himself, he began to turn from the theatre to poetry, and the following decade saw the writing of those poems for which he is now chiefly famous. There are the great satires, *Absalom and Achitophel* (1681), *The Medal* (1682) and *MacFlecknoe* (1682), which respond to the public events of the last years of King Charles' reign; and not only these, but the two long religious poems which give a public face to Dryden's more private concerns about belief, *Religio Laici* (1682) and *The Hind and the Panther* (1687).

Dryden was still an Anglican when he wrote the earlier of these two poems, still able to echo and argue for the prevailing Restoration consensus about religion. It is impossible to know what drove him from this to Roman Catholicism, perhaps a coincidence of the most internal reasons, domestic reasons (his wife and sons may already have been Catholics when he wrote *Religio Laici*) and public reasons (the Catholic James II had succeeded Charles II in 1685). At any rate, by 1686 Dryden was a Catholic, and the stage was set for that separation from the mainstream of the Restoration settlement, after the fall of James II in 1688, which marked the last twelve years of his life. He lost the laureateship and turned again, reluctantly, to the theatre for money with *Don Sebastian* (1690) and *Amphitryon* (1690), a tragedy and a comedy to parallel *Marriage A-la-Mode* and *All for Love*. Again for money, he began translating, contemplating perhaps the fact that he had commenced writer in London for Herringman by providing short prefaces for a translation by his Cambridge friend Francis Gifford.

Dryden may have been short of money again as he had been in 1657, but now he was the most famous poet in England, and his translation of *The Works of Virgil* (1697) and *Fables Ancient and*

Modern (1700) from Homer, Ovid, Boccacio and Chaucer added to his fame. No longer at the heart of public political affairs, he was nevertheless by now a great enough man to create his own public and to preside amid a great number of friends and followers. These were not only old men like himself, for perhaps the most striking friendship of the last years of Dryden's life was with the young Congreve, whom Dryden looked upon as another son, and who wrote brilliantly for the stage in the last decade of the century, but wrote no more after Dryden's death. The old poet must have been pleased, like Falstaff in *2 Henry IV*, to be not only witty but the cause of wit in other men (I. ii), for he was in these years long past combative satire. He died in the spring of 1700, and seventeen years later Congreve published the complete edition of his plays that is quoted with the siglum D in this edition. Words from Congreve's prefatory memoir are a good epitaph, prologue into good epilogue:

> He was of a Nature exceedingly Humane and Compassionate; easily forgiving Injuries, and capable of a prompt and sincere Reconciliation with them who had offended him...He was not more possess'd of Knowledge than he was Communicative of it. But then his Communication of it was by no means pedantick, or impos'd upon the Conversation...He was extream ready and gentle in his Correction of the Errors of any Writer, who thought fit to consult him; and full as ready and patient to admit of the Reprehension of others in respect of his own Oversight or Mistakes...I may venture to say in general Terms, that no Man hath written in our Language so much, and so various Matter, and in so various Manners, so well.

THE CONTEXT OF THE PLAY

In June and July of 1671 the king was at Windsor (see note at Dedication 8) in the company, among others, of the Duke of Buckingham and the Earl of Rochester; and for some part of the time Dryden was invited to be present. It must have been an overwhelming experience for the distinctly less aristocratic poet who was nevertheless the most successful playwright in the kingdom. Dryden clearly had with him on this visit the manuscript of *Marriage À-la-Mode*, complete or almost complete, because he described in the later dedication of the play to Rochester how well it had been received by King Charles and how greatly the king's liking had contributed to its subsequent success on the stage.

Dryden's reaction to being taken up by great men, and indeed their own treatment of him, was ambivalent. There was about him always a strain of extreme diffidence, to the very end of his life (Congreve remarked upon it in his memoir), and to judge from the tone of the Dedication (lines 15–46), Dryden was as much repelled by the stupidity and pettiness of court life as he was flattered by the attention of a few great ones. Not only the Dedication of *Marriage A-la-Mode* but the play itself reflects this duality. Dryden was uneasy as well as excited, and events in fact justified his unease, for Rochester's capricious favour was soon attracted to other writers and away from him, and Buckingham was at this precise time in the process of converting an earlier satirical sketch about ludicrous ranting plays into an attack upon Dryden, and taking the opportunity of making it spectacularly focussed and up-to-date: when Buckingham's play *The Rehearsal* was first performed at the Theatre Royal, Drury Lane, on 7 December 1671, the appropriately named playwright-hero, Bayes, was manifestly the poet laureate, and among the plays by Dryden parodied was *Marriage A-la-Mode*, a new piece for the same theatre. It was true, and Dryden makes much of it in his play (see notes at Prologue 24, III. i. 110, IV. iii. 190 and IV. iv. 123–6), that the audience at the Theatre Royal was royalist in sympathy, but Dryden the great apologist for king and court, for the elegance of France, for polish and wit in conversation, could also be satirised there, outmanoeuvred by those who, unlike him, were socially the genuine aristocratic article, and confident enough of themselves to make it brutally clear that they had no need of his enthusiasm. The king had been aware when he made Dryden poet laureate that a writer of this stature on the king's side was worth having; but the general court reaction to Dryden's excited defence of their style of life was no doubt cooler, at least in the poet's absence. He was not one of them, nor about to become one of them by such means. Dryden must have felt much of this (see note on the title page quotation from Horace), and we see in *Marriage A-la-Mode* a complication of attitude towards courts and towards social climbing that arises from his perplexity.

It is not clear whether the first performance of *Marriage A-la-Mode* took place before or after *The Rehearsal* (see note at Dedication 2). The earliest date for a production must be the beginning of the 1671–2 theatrical season, and more specifically 9 November 1671, because the opening of the new Dorset Garden Theatre seems to be alluded to in the Prologue (see note at Prologue 24). The latest date for a first performance is probably 25 February 1672, because after the destruction of the Theatre Royal on that day and the move to temporary quarters at the Duke's Company's old theatre in Lincoln's Inn Fields, references in the Prologue to the distance a city audience would have to travel to see the play would seem rather less compelling, though it would still certainly be true that the Dorset Garden Theatre was a closer and more spectacular attraction.

In the absence of more specific evidence, a date for the first production of *Marriage A-la-Mode* in the week or two preceding *The Rehearsal* seems most likely. One could hardly imagine that the King's Company would be slow to put on a play specifically commended by the king; and it seems just as likely that Buckingham would have wanted his own play to follow upon the heels of Dryden's as closely as possible, so that not only would the audience pick up and relish tiny details of satiric comment on a play recently performed by many of the same actors, but also the actors themselves, in rehearsing and performing *The Rehearsal*, would have the rehearsing and performing of *Marriage A-la-Mode* freshly in mind. It is, after all, a common experience in rehearsal that the more acute rhetorical angles of any serious play are often first perceived as funny, that this is the way they attract energy to themselves; and the serious plot of Dryden's half-comic, half-serious play would have provided the actors with many moments – some matters of the words spoken but many others, no doubt, matters of tiny detail of dress, movement or tone – that emerged in performance on the serious side of the line dividing them from farce, but that were fruitfully recalled as farcical for the purposes of Buckingham's play. The very close relationship we can imagine between Dryden's play and Buckingham's comes to seem very like the relationship between serious and comic elements in *Marriage A-la-Mode* itself, not a damaging conflict so much as a strangely fruitful collaboration. Dryden, after all, was a shareholder in the King's Company and would have profited financially as much by the success of Buckingham's play as his own. It must have been good, too, to be famous enough to be satirised.

THE PLAY

Marriage A-la-Mode is a play, as I have said, half-comic and half-serious, and it has been usual to suggest that it is as a comedy that it really succeeds. The title seems to refer one chiefly to the comic plot consisting of the two couples, Doralice-Rhodophil and Melantha-Palamede, the first couple married, the second about to be married, who intrigue across the boundaries in temporary alliances as Doralice-Palamede and Melantha-Rhodophil. The comic plot (which has also, it should be said, darker elements lurking within it; see note at IV. iii. 111) is attached only lightly in formal structural terms to the serious, heroic plot which presents us with another foursome, the true and constant lovers, Palmyra-Leonidas, and their respective fathers, the usurping king, Polydamas, and the rightful king, Theagenes, who is dead before the play begins. The two young people have been brought up secretly away from the court and it is at first thought that Leonidas is Polydamas' son, then suddenly revealed that the reverse is the case, that it is Palmyra who is his child, and Leonidas the rightful king in succession to Theagenes. The various reversals of social fortune undergone by Leonidas and Palmyra test but do not shake their true love. Even though they have to live in the court world with its oppressive social assumptions and assertive language, and though they acquiesce to some degree in it, they are privately concerned to exclude that world, its language and attitudes, whereas the couples in the comic plot acquiesce wholly in this language, in the standards accepted in court life, and Melantha strives desperately for proficiency in it, as the chief indicator of human worth.

There are structural parallels between the two plots in the patterns of relationship and change of relationship, but the absence of strong structural links between them, the difference in atmosphere between them, extending even to the invariable prose of the comic plot and verse of the serious plot, early invited a simplified understanding of the play which led to its being played solely as comedy, with the heroic part cut completely. The last early performance of the full text of the play took place seven months after Dryden's death, in November 1700, and by 1703 there was an anonymous adaptation which turned the play into a two-act comic piece. Further adaptations in the eighteenth century concentrated on the comic plot, emphasising steadily more and more the role of Melantha, the frenchified lady. The eighteenth-century versions were often called *Marriage A-la-Mode*, but, as I hope to show, they are not. Dryden's original play is in fact very much a unity, a strange and complex unity held together by forces operating more subtly than at the structural level, responding to Dryden's own ambivalence about formal, public social life, life with its wig on rather than its Indian gown (see note at III. i. 230), and enabling us better perhaps than any other Restoration play to think deeply about the proper place of public life, public wit, publicly contrived relationship in the whole spectrum of human experience.

We begin with the court in *Marriage A-la-Mode*, which provides in structural terms the chief area of overlap between the two plots. The dominant feature of court life is the ease and self-confidence of those who move within its boundaries, an ease which expresses itself in various ways, in the witty repartee of the two gay couples of the comic plot, in the peremptory authority of the king, Polydamas, and in the way in which first Leonidas and then Palmyra undergo partial changes of character which press in upon and have to seek accommodation with their former innocent character as pastoral lovers when it is discovered that they are insiders not outsiders in court terms. The boundaries of this court life are clearly set in the play, in satiric terms in the comic plot (see for instance III. i. 106–66 and IV. iii. 128–34), where the town, the city and the country are the ever darker circles of hell beyond its light; and in pastoral terms in the serious plot (see for instance II. i. 401–97), where Leonidas and Palmyra recall their country life before they came to court and give a very different picture of the country from that given in satiric terms. We should remember that Dryden always loved the country (see p. ix) and was himself a town-man, or more accurately perhaps a kind of Melantha figure, stranded a little desperately across the boundary line between the court and the world beyond: and if we have this in mind it becomes easy to account for the fact that the invasive pressure upon the boundary line of the court from outside is characterised in *Marriage A-la-Mode* both as laughable, with the town-ladies crowding in and sweating on holiday-nights (III. i. 109–10), and as dangerously innocent, genuine, alive, with Palmyra and Leonidas recalling the birth and growth of the now unbreakable bond between them, and making the court all round them look cheap and tawdry. Palmyra speaks here:

> I know too well when first my love began.
> When, at our wake, you for the chaplet ran.
> Then I was made the lady of the May,
> And with the garland at the goal did stay.
> Still as you ran, I kept you full in view;
> I hoped, and wished, and ran, methought, for you.   (II. i. 426–31)

There seems more genuine nobility about Palmyra's country grandeur, because youth, innocence, love and truth accompany her as 'lady of the May' (as with Perdita in *The Winter's Tale;* see note at III. i. 297), than about the nobility found in the court. The point is made in a particularly telling way when Polydamas condemns her, at III. i. 297–305 to the shame of being a pageant queen as part of the ritual of her execution. Polydamas is himself not the rightful king, he is deceived in thinking Leonidas and not Palmyra is his child, he sets true love well below his fancied honour: so that at the centre of the court there is found an old, corrupt, deceived and loveless king. The pressure upon the court from the external pastoral source reveals the court as itself a deeply flawed place; and we may well think the laughable pressure upon it from the town-ladies is only in the end like seeking like, as we contemplate, in stark contrast to the pastoral love of Palmyra and Leonidas, the intense, loveless competition for place that occupies the thoughts of those born and bred within its boundaries. Love is constantly talked about in the witty exchanges between Rhodophil, Palamede, Doralice and Melantha; but it is a competitive, negotiable commodity kept in an appearance of life only by relentless wit. The wit is very amusing, very skilled, very quick; it is also very, very tiring; and the stillness and security of the love between Leonidas and Palmyra give the audience clear respite from the constant shower of wit that dances about them during the comic parts of the play.

In different but complementary ways, then, the energies deriving from the comic and serious plots allow us to contemplate the court's shortcomings. But this is not the whole story. There hovers about the whole play a persistent sense almost of the divinity of kingship, that requires nothing in the way of complementary merit, honour or virtue to give it force. If a man is said to be a king (and by extension if his child is said to be his child, his courtier said to be his courtier) then that social divinity settles upon him. The point is emphatically made when we are told early in the play, at I. i. 245-74, that Polydamas is not the lawful king, and shown Palamede, a few lines later on, at I. i. 316-25, swearing loyalty like a true subject to his noble king, Polydamas. Palamede, unlike the audience and others in the court, knows nothing of how Polydamas seized the throne; but it is inevitable that the audience themselves here feel the full strain of the situation upon them, as they are given no choice but to acquiesce in Palamede's noble sentiments and thus in Polydamas' status as king, setting aside the force of what they have just heard. Kingship has settled upon Polydamas, and until it is taken away right at the end of the play, it has its deifying effect. Kingship is necessary to the life of this play (without it there would be no secure foundation for the consciously courtly wit of the two gay couples in the comic plot) and it is necessary, too, to the life of the audience; so necessary that the worth of the man said to be king is a secondary consideration. Dryden understood much better than Buckingham or Rochester that, although they were the genuine article in a way that he was not (see p. xii), they were nevertheless aristocrats not as the result of some individual inevitable natural process, but because they were *necessary;* and if not they, then some other convenient men. One wonders whether Buckingham stirred uneasily in his seat as he watched Polydamas on the stage, in spite of the airy confidence with which he was about to put Dryden himself on the stage as Bayes. Dryden had the last word in the passage of arms with the duke when he portrayed him as Zimri in *Absalom and Achitophel* ten years later, but he was not without teeth even in *Marriage A-la-Mode*.

Kingship in this play, then, and so also the court, as a central social necessity, mirrors its status in the real life of the audience. Once this is granted – once it is granted that a king is king, or a courtier a courtier, because in the abstract there has to be a king and a court, and not because these particular human beings are by nature peculiarly kingly or courtly – then the play can work towards a sense of the kind of individual character *desirable* in a king or a courtier. In the midst of all the witty repartee of Doralice, Palamede, Melantha and Rhodophil, and in the midst of the serious intrigue revolving round Polydamas, Leonidas and Palmyra, there emerges as the play comes to an end an individual, Leonidas, who is not only the necessary but the legitimate king, and who is merciful, magnanimous, noble and devoted to his true love, Palmyra. Leonidas and Palmyra accept the necessary reality of kingship and in the course of the play negotiate an alliance between it and their own private virtue. At the end of the comic plot, too, the temporary intriguing alliances between the four witty lovers resolve themselves into the patterns of true love and stable marriage as Doralice-Rhodophil and Melantha-Palamede. It becomes possible to be both courtly, witty and married. The end, then, of the comic plot only avoids anti-climax (of a kind jokingly suggested when the Epilogue speaks of the audience's frustration that illicit sex has not occurred) and instead makes substantial sense if we consider it in close relationship with the serious plot.

In some subtle way, while writing this play, Dryden drew both upon his sense of king and court as the fundamental social magic and upon his intense uneasiness about court life. Like one of those pictures that alters completely when presented at a different angle to the eye, *Marriage A-la-Mode* restlessly switches between tones in its complex attempt to do justice to the whole spectrum of Dryden's opinion, and it rouses us to a similar complexity of response. In a particularly emphatic way the role of Melantha, the frenchified town-lady aspiring to be a courtier, together with the frenchified English she speaks, is a focus of shifting tonal patterns. I have suggested before that Melantha is in some ways a kind of Dryden figure (see p. xv), certainly more accurately Dryden than Bayes could be, and this may help us to be unsurprised that she is the most intense locus of linguistic energy in the play. Melantha is utterly self-absorbed, quite unaware that the world operates in other than public terms, and so keenly aware of the magic of kingship that her reactions to Leonidas and Palmyra as they are successively royal and not royal flick over in instant response to the

newly revealed state of affairs. She is the most sensitively calibrated
and responsive instrument in the play for the recording of social
change. When she changes allegiance as the fortunes of Leonidas or
Palmyra rise or fall, we and others in the play laugh at her; but it is
just that she changes more quickly than either we or they do
(though not more quickly than Polydamas himself). She is a fool,
then, but not a fool, for she understands the divinity of kingship
better than the courtiers who smile at her. We and they smile, too,
at her extraordinary speech, stuffed full as it is of French words and
expressions. It is true that her speech is ludicrous, artificially
contrived to an extreme degree, her new lines learnt before every
fresh performance like some actress on the stage; true also that she
can on occasion give a performance that is disastrously inappro-
priate to the condition of the world about her (see V. i. 80–127), like
playing comedy during the plague. But her performances are in
themselves brilliant; she takes hold of the lurking energy of
enthusiasm for things French to be found everywhere in the court
(just as she takes hold of the enthusiasm for actresses to be found
everywhere in the audience), and reveals in a bravura performance
just how exciting artifice can be. At a climactic moment near the
end of the play (V. i. 124–86), she arouses in Palamede and Philotis
their own latent Frenchness, so that all three are stirred to a weirdly
intense pitch of excitement as the two languages pass across each
other and attract each other, linguistic strangers closely embracing,
in a way that is not far from physical lust, which is also in its turn a
familiar of that sudden sense of strangeness made intimate that we
call nakedness.

Dryden was nakedly conscious of language as Melantha is, and
as with her his nakedness sometimes embarrasses and sometimes
excites us, sometimes both at the same time, as when in the
Dedication he compares Rochester to God (see lines 81–4 and
note), which is after all what a dedicatee is. Perhaps Rochester
stirred uneasily at this point, as I have imagined Buckingham
stirring at the portrayal of Polydamas (see p. xvi), wondering
whether Dryden was not more intelligently aware of the range of
reality, its splendours and idiocies, than he was. If it is true, as
Dryden says in his Dedication (lines 15–22), that the easy
interchange of witty conversation in the comic parts of this play,
and the delicacies and decencies of the serious parts, owe much to
Rochester's speech and manner, then in some way Rochester has
fathered not only the ordinary tenor of *Marriage A-la-Mode* but also
its extreme moments.

Melantha is in a constant state of excitement in *Marriage A-la-
Mode* because she desires but does not possess the life of the court.
Those who live within the charmed circle are cooler about it; they

do not sweat for introduction like the town-ladies (III. i. 109–18). The court is in some way more exciting, more magic, when one does not belong. Almost its major social function is to be unattainable. And so our sense of the glories of kingship derives more emphatically from those who are remote from it than those who are close. If the court would be glorious, the town-ladies are essential to it, and their risible antics are vital to its serious sense of its own weight and importance. If there were no town-ladies, then nevertheless the court would have to assume that those outside were town-ladies beneath the skin. In a similar way in this play, the delights of sexual love are alluringly felt when they are not had. Desire is the product of frustration; so that marriage, with the permission it gives desire, is the death of it.

Doralice-Palamede and Melantha-Rhodophil sweat for copulation as the town-ladies sweat for a sight of royalty, and the hectic activity of their witty speech is as much a struggle to press close to the charmed circle of fulfilled desire as the struggles of the crowd on holiday-nights. Desire, however, offers golden fruit that abruptly seems dust and ashes when it is grasped. All the comic parts of this play operate with just such desire, and as it were they seek salvation from it; for a witty play cannot go on being witty without breeding deadly fatigue, in characters and audience alike, but neither, in its own terms, can it come to successful conclusion without anti-climax, dust and ashes. It is, as I have said, the serious part of the play which allows the comic part a substantially significant end, which is neither the anti-climax of illicit desire still unattained (see p. xvii), nor that of illicit desire achieved, nor that of dully accepted marriage; and this is because the relationship of Palmyra and Leonidas opens the possibility that desire achieved might breed more desire, the possibility that steadily experienced sexual love has deep within it the fount of energetic, striving life. If that is so, then marriage loses its terrors; and if Leonidas and Palmyra, as king and queen, really love each other in this constantly fresh arising of desire, then they may also transform the divinity of kingship settled upon them, for so long as it consents to remain; for then perhaps the court too, and its whole witty social life, may become a place that does not need to draw upon the external energy of those who envy it from outside. For a moment, at the end of the play, it seems there is presented the radically idealistic possibility that neither the courts of kings nor the loves of lovers need any social context of other human envy and frustration to give them life. The king is in this view most fully king when he has no subjects, the court most fully a court when no one (like Dryden) need feel excluded.

Because of the deep inconsistency of attitudes it accommodates,

Marriage A-la-Mode invites such speculation, and it is in the uneasiness of the tonal mix in the play that we may find its chief and substantial originality. The sources upon which Dryden drew in constructing his play and furnishing it with attitudes are much what one would expect, but what he draws into his play from these sources is there made complex and unexpected, uneasy and original. The chief source for the serious plot is to be found in Madeleine de Scudéry's vast heroic romance, which appeared in ten volumes between 1649 and 1653, *Artamène: ou le Grand Cyrus*. This appeared in five volumes in English translation between 1653 and 1655 and was phenomenally popular (Pepys had to rebuke his wife on 11 May 1666 for continually telling stories from *The Grand Cyrus*). The serious plot of *Marriage A-la-Mode* is essentially the story of 'Sesostris and Timareta' from *The Grand Cyrus*, with Sesostris renamed Leonidas and Timareta renamed Palmyra, the other characters also given new names, and the whole thing greatly condensed and sharpened into dramatic action.

The comic plot has sources more popular, more commonplace still. 'The History of Timantes and Parthenia' from *The Grand Cyrus* gives us a married courtier and a bachelor who may remind us of Rhodophil and Palamede in their attitudes to love and marriage: but really, as the California editors memorably put it (p. 470): 'plots involving masquerading wives and fashionable opinion that, to quote an old French song, "les baisers permis sont fades" could be had for the asking on any street corner of the Strand or Saint Germain'.

Dryden had himself dramatised such opinions about love and marriage before, in *The Wild Gallant* (1663) and *The Rival Ladies* (1664), and he is indeed himself one of the conspicuous sources for *Marriage A-la-Mode*. The character of Melantha may well, as L. H. Martin suggests ('The Source and Originality of Dryden's Melantha', *PQ* 53 (1973), 746–53) derive from Berisa in *The Grand Cyrus*, but there is a preliminary sketch for Melantha and Philotis in the scenes between Aurelia and Camilla in *An Evening's Love* (1668). A song from *An Evening's Love* also makes its way into *Marriage A-la-Mode* (see note at III. i. 140), and the alternating of comic and serious plots is paralleled in *Secret Love* (1667).

Two other playwrights, Molière and Shakespeare, make their impress upon the play. There are songs from *Le Bourgeois Gentilhomme* in Act V (see note at V. i. 150–1), and several of Shakespeare's plays are fragmentarily echoed. *The Winter's Tale*, set in Sicily like *Marriage A-la-Mode*, must have been in Dryden's mind as he described the pastoral love of Leonidas and Palmyra (see notes at II. i. 401 and III. i. 297). From the beginning and the end of *All's Well That Ends Well* there are momentary hints (see notes at I. i. 317, I. i. 438 and III. i. 462–3). There is a reminiscence of *Romeo and Juliet* in the masking scene in Act IV (see note at IV. ii. 9); and there are specific references to *Antony and Cleopatra* and *Macbeth* (see notes at III. i. 325 and V. i. 372).

The impression left, especially by these last uses of *Antony and Cleopatra* and *Macbeth*, of a play rather randomly picking up fairly standard literary and theatrical elements may usefully emphasise for us the looseness of the structural weave in *Marriage A-la-Mode*. The play arises from a mind stocked with social, literary and theatrical experience, and it explores relationships between elements that do not fit neatly together in Dryden's understanding. I hope now to suggest how far the loose texture of *Marriage A-la-Mode* made it a play ideally suited for the Restoration stage.

THE STAGING OF THE PLAY

Perhaps the first thing a modern audience would be aware of if suddenly transported to a Restoration theatre would be that they were not sitting in darkness during the performance. The stage and the auditorium are lit by the same chandeliers. The play taking place is not drawing the audience into a hypnotic cocoon of illusion, as on the modern stage, where for the duration of the action the only world is the world of the play, which must as a consequence cohere together closely, be as well knit together as any other world which is to survive as a distinct entity. Instead, audience, players and characters alike share a larger illusory world, the world of the playhouse itself (which in its turn is not very remote from the world outside), in which the play being performed is no more than the chief element. The boundary line between play and audience is certainly clear, as between the court in *Marriage A-la-Mode* and the town-ladies outside pressing in to see the show, but it is much more easily crossed than that social divide. For one thing, the whole idea of public life in London as well-dressed spectacle is so familiar to the audience that the well-dressed (and similarly dressed – with even shepherds in perukes; see note at I. i. 356+) spectacle on the stage seems no more than a heightening of the theatricality of life outside the playhouse. In terms of the playhouse geography itself, too, the forestage projecting well into the auditorium, on which most of the action takes place, allows the players a very intimate, conversational relationship with the audience, a relationship exploited to the full, not only in the frequent use of asides, as in this play, but in other non-verbal appeals beyond the world of the play by looks and gestures. The elaborately 'theatrical' language of gesture which formed a major part of Restoration acting technique was plainly too large for the world of the play considered as a real world existing in its own terms, and was instead meant to speak across the boundary line to an audience assumed to be itself a more distant part of the same play.

The totality of play experience being offered, then, in *Marriage A-la-Mode* is more extensive and complex than what we read in the verbal notation we call the play. We have seen already that the play Dryden wrote arose from much more than its literary sources or literary imaginings. We can understand, as a consequence, why it seems quite in order to treat what is said in the Dedication of the printed text, not to speak of the play's Prologue and Epilogue, as part of the total plot; just as Buckingham's play *The Rehearsal* is a kind of complicating coda. We can see now, too, how appropriate to the conditions of the contemporary stage it is that the play as written seems to offer us a series of rather isolated moments, of serious high drama, sudden revelation, or witty exchange, each one intensely engaged in, as though what is before and after is for a moment forgotten (the most striking of these perhaps being Palamede's homage to a king just revealed as a usurper; see p. xvi). The subtlety of Dryden's play is meant to come to life in the audience's own attempts to hold together the slightly loosely assembled parts: as though Dryden were saying to the audience, 'You reacted well to that, did you? And you reacted well to that other moment? Well, how do you account for the inconsistency? We live, do we not, in a complicated world, all of us?' It is as though the main line of music notated in the play's text has rests and pauses in it, during which we should hear accompanying parts played from the auditorium. We may imagine that they whistled or sang in response to the songs in the play (rather like the household audience at III. i. 137–45 in response to another of Dryden's songs); and similarly we should envisage a much more lively, debate-like response to the other high moments than would occur with a modern audience. The modern audience is more used to hearing the whole piece, orchestration and all; they expect the irony of the Palamede-Polydamas situation to be accommodated within what is spoken on the stage, rather than to supply it from the sketched-out notation provided by the playwright.

This notion of *Marriage A-la-Mode* as total theatre may help us to understand also the *explicitness* of everything that is said in the play (contrast the dramatic method of Congreve, who read *Marriage A-la-Mode* carefully when writing *The Way of the World*). The play is not without subtlety, as I have argued, and it is certainly not without *double entendre* and disguise. But everything in the play is meant to be *instantly understood*, at the moment it is said, by the audience. There is nothing hidden away from the audience behind what the characters say. When they feel something, they say it, and that is what they feel. We look in vain in *Marriage A-la-Mode* for levels of scarcely understood, scarcely acknowledgeable possibility behind words spoken. By comparison with the characters of Shakespeare, these are cardboard cut-outs. And the players act the parts with the large, stylised gestures appropriate to characters whose total life is securely expressible in an external gesture or word. But Dryden knew what he was doing. The characters are like the events of the play; isolation and explicitness go hand in hand. Each one of the characters is a high moment, and it is the Restoration audience that must bring to life, in the space provided between each character, the weave of private subtlety that in any world that is to hang together must criss-cross the spaces between public actors on the stage of life.

Marriage A-la-Mode, because it is not simply a comedy, makes more energetic use, I think, of the total acting capacity of the Restoration theatre, players and audience alike, than a simple comedy would. The dislocations are more glaring, the gaps larger, the audience must work harder at its weaving. It was to be expected, perhaps, that as time passed and audiences changed, both in the kind of experience they expected in the theatre and in the world they ordinarily lived in, Dryden's play should seem less and less a possible unity, so that a radical simplification became necessary by the cutting away of the serious plot. Moral objections, too, to the sexuality of the play, besides being one impetus clearly behind the steadily increasing concentration on Melantha's frenchified speech and manner, a safe comic arena, in the eighteenth century, must have ensured its disappearance from the stage in the nineteenth.

With the productions of the English Stage Society and the Phoenix Society, and the more commercial efforts of Nigel Playfair at the Lyric Theatre, Hammersmith, in the 1920s, Restoration comedy in general began to enjoy a revival. There were moral objections to be overcome, and an audience to be re-educated. J. L. Styan (*Restoration Comedy in Performance*, p. 246) quotes Norman Marshall on Nigel Playfair's experience at the Lyric:

> When he began his work at the Lyric the whole technique of acting and production in England was based on a pretence of ignoring the audience and isolating the actors in their own world behind the footlights. Playfair's method was to accept the presence of the audience, to make them a partner in the play, and to establish a feeling of intimacy between the stage and auditorium.

It was in this kind of atmosphere that *Marriage A-la-Mode* was revived in 1920 by the Phoenix Society. (The *Spectator* reviewer on

17 January 1920 found it exceedingly unedifying). There were further revivals in 1928 at the Birmingham Repertory Theatre and the Festival Theatre, Cambridge; and in 1946 at the St James Theatre, directed by John Clements. This last production ran for less than a month and failed essentially because Clements could not keep the serious and comic parts of the play together. It seems that he tried to combine these different elements by imposing a uniform comic tone overall (not by any subtler understanding of the play's unity) and that 'the production unraveled accordingly' (Retta M. Taney, *Restoration Revivals on the British Stage, 1944–1979* (1985), pp. 70–1).

THE TEXT

A copy of the first printed version of *Marriage A-la-Mode*, by T. N. for Henry Herringman, 1673, now in the Huntington Library (122840), provides the copy text for this edition. The text is almost free of difficulty, but a few readings have been accepted from later editions of the play: Q2 (1684), Q3 (1691), Q4 (1698), F (Dryden's *Comedies, Tragedies, and Operas*, 1701) and D (Dryden's *Dramatick Works*, 1717). Readings accepted from the California *Dryden* are marked 'ed.', and the copy of Q1 used as copy text by the California editors is occasionally cited, with the siglum Q1a. The italicisation of the copy text for this edition has been modernised; but it is preserved as in the original where it is used to highlight words immediately derived from French or still felt as not necessarily naturalised English speech, particularly in Melantha's affected style. Where I have felt it necessary to regularise this typographical practice with French words, a textual note records the fact. The matter is not altogether simple, because at times it is not clear whether what seems anomalous practice is a printer's error or an indication that contemporary judgement of the English status of a word, the degree to which it was French or could be frenchified, differed from our own. Spelling, punctuation and capitalisation by contrast present little difficulty and have been silently modernised, except in a few cases, as where there is no satisfactory modern equivalent of a word. The spelling of French words has been similarly treated, without any textual note except where the spelling in the copy text clearly could not be correct contemporary usage. Where changes to the copy text are recorded in the notes, only the minimum necessary authority is given for the preferred reading.

FURTHER READING

The standard modern edition of *Marriage A-la-Mode* is to be found in *The Works of John Dryden*, vol. 11, ed. John Loftis, David S. Rodes et al. (University of California Press, Berkeley, 1978).

Modern biographies of Dryden include Charles E. Ward, *The Life of John Dryden* (Chapel Hill, 1961); and there are useful critical approaches to the plays in Frank H. Moore, *The Nobler Pleasure: Dryden's Comedy in Theory and Practice* (Chapel Hill, 1963); and general critical reading on Dryden should include Earl Miner, *Dryden's Poetry* (Bloomington, 1967)

For the general critical background the following works should be consulted; J. Harrington Smith, *The Gay Couple in Restoration Comedy* (Cambridge, Mass., 1948); Robert D. Hume, *The Development of English Drama in the Late Seventeenth Century* (Oxford, 1976); Jocelyn Powell, *Restoration Theatre Production* (London, 1984); J. L. Styan, *Restoration Comedy in Performance* (Cambridge, 1986); Nancy K. Maguire, *Regicide and Restoration: English Tragicomedy 1660-1671* (Cambridge, 1992); Gillian Manning, *Libertine Plays of the Restoration* (London, 2001); and *A Companion to Restoration Drama*, ed. Susan J. Owen (Oxford, 2001). Useful works on the background of theatrical history include: John Loftis et al., *The Revels History of Drama in English*, vol. 5 (London, 1976); *The London Theatre World, 1660-1806*, ed. Robet D. Hume (Carbondale, 1980); and Derek Hughes, *English Drama 1660-1700* (Oxford, 1996).

MARRIAGE
A-la-Mode.

A
COMEDY.

As it is Acted at the

THEATRE-ROYAL.

Written by *JOHN DRYDEN*, Servant
to His Majesty.

——————— *Quicquid sum ego, quamvis*
Infra Lucilli censum ingeniumque, tamen me
Cum magnis vixisse, invita fatebitur usque
Invidia, & fragili quærens illidere dentem
Offendet solido.

Horat. Serm.

LONDON,

Printed by *T. N.* for *Henry Herringman*, and are to be
sold at the *Anchor* in the Lower Walk of
the *New Exchange.* 1673.

Photo: the Huntington Library, San Marino, California

Servant...Majesty. Dryden was made poet laureate in April 1668.

Quicquid...solido. The passage is from Horace, *Satires* II. i. 74–9: 'Such as I am, though in inherited property and native wit less than Lucillus, envy will nevertheless unwillingly confess this much, that I have at least lived with the great, and if she tries to get her teeth into me as a delicate little morsel, she will find I am hard to bite on.' Horace is defending himself against attack for criticising some verses by the poet Lucillus; and Dryden clearly quotes the passage as a way of alluding to pamphlet attacks on his own play *The Conquest of Granada* (printed 1672.) The pamphlets appeared in the spring of 1673. Dryden refers again to this passage from Horace in his preface to *The Assignation*, also printed in 1673. In the dedication to Rochester that now follows, Dryden represents himself, accurately, as one with some experience of the court, though not a great man himself; Horace was perhaps in his mind.

To the Right Honourable,
The EARL of
ROCHESTER

My Lord,

I humbly dedicate to your Lordship that poem, of which you were pleased to appear an early patron, before it was acted on the stage. I may yet go farther, with your permission, and say, that it received amendment from your noble hands, ere it was fit to be presented. You may please likewise to   5
remember with how much favour to the author and indulgence to the play you commended it to the view of His Majesty, then at Windsor, and by his approbation of it in writing, made way for its kind reception on the theatre. In this Dedication, therefore, I may seem to imitate a custom of   10
the ancients, who offered to their gods the firstlings of the flock, which I think they called *ver sacrum*, because they helped them to increase. I am sure, if there be anything in this play wherein I have raised myself beyond the ordinary lowness of my comedies, I ought wholly to acknowledge it   15
to the favour of being admitted into your Lordship's conversation. And not only I, who pretend not to this way, but the best comic writers of our age, will join with me to acknowledge that they have copied the gallantries of courts, the delicacy of expression, and the decencies of behaviour   20
from your Lordship with more success than if they had taken their models from the court of France. But this, my Lord, will be no wonder to the world, which knows the excellency of your natural parts, and those you have acquired in a noble education. That which with more reason I admire is that,   25

ROCHESTER The poet John Wilmot, 2nd Earl of Rochester (1647–80)

2 *before it was acted* The first record of a performance of *Marriage A-la-Mode* dates from April 1674, but it is clear that the play must actually have been first performed in the theatrical season of 1671–2, quite soon after it had attracted the special notice of the king. See pp. xii–xiii and notes at Dedication 8 and Prologue 24.

8 *then at Windsor* King Charles was at Windsor from 26 May to 13 July 1671.

12 *ver sacrum* literally, 'holy spring'. The custom was to sacrifice animals born in the spring to a god, to ensure his favour. The ancients acknowledged the help of the gods as Dryden acknowledges Rochester's help.

17 *who pretend not to this way* Dryden always asserted that he wrote comedy only in response to public demand, and not from any ambition to be a comic dramatist.

being so absolute a courtier, you have not forgot either the
ties of friendship or the practice of generosity. In my little
experience of a court (which I confess I desire not to improve)
I have found in it much of interest and more of detraction.
Few men there have that assurance of a friend as not to be   30
made ridiculous by him when they are absent. There are
a middling sort of courtiers who become happy by their want
of wit, but they supply that want by an excess of malice to
those who have it. And there is no such persecution as that of
fools: they can never be considerable enough to be talked of   35
themselves, so that they are safe only in their obscurity, and
grow mischievous to witty men by the great diligence of their
envy, and by being always present to represent and aggravate
their faults. In the mean time they are forced, when they
endeavour to be pleasant, to live on the offals of their wit,   40
whom they decry, and either to quote it (which they do
unwillingly) or to pass it upon others for their own. These are
the men who make it their business to chase wit from the
knowledge of princes, lest it should disgrace their ignorance.
And this kind of malice your Lordship has not so much   45
avoided as surmounted. But if by the excellent temper of a
royal master, always more ready to hear good than ill, if by his
inclination to love you, if by your own merit and address, if
by the charms of your conversation, the grace of your
behaviour, your knowledge of greatness and habitude in   50
courts, you have been able to preserve yourself with honour
in the midst of so dangerous a course; yet at least the
remembrance of those hazards has inspired you with pity for
other men who, being of an inferior wit and quality to you,
are yet persecuted for being that in little which your Lordship   55
is in great. For the quarrel of those people extends itself to
anything of sense and, if I may be so vain to own it amongst
the rest of the poets, has sometimes reached to the very
borders of it, even to me. So that, if our general good fortune
had not raised up your Lordship to defend us, I know not   60
whether anything had been more ridiculous in court than
writers. 'Tis to your Lordship's favour we generally owe our
protection and patronage, and to the nobleness of your

51 *have* F (having Q1)

---

29 *interest* self-interest
32 *middling sort* The three kinds of courtier are the 'absolute' (line 26), the 'middling'
    and the 'fools' (line 35). The 'middling sort' flourish parasitically on the witty
    energy of those better than they, whereas the 'fools' seem less sprightly in the
    'diligence' (line 37) of their envy.

nature, which will not suffer the least shadow of your wit to
be contemned in other men. You have been often pleased not 65
only to excuse my imperfections but to vindicate what was
tolerable in my writings from their censures. And what I
never can forget, you have not only been careful of my
reputation but of my fortune. You have been solicitous to
supply my neglect of myself; and to overcome the fatal 70
modesty of poets, which submits them to perpetual wants
rather than to become importunate with those people who
have the liberality of kings in their disposing; and who,
dishonouring the bounty of their master, suffer such to be in
necessity who endeavour at least to please him, and for whose 75
entertainment he has generously provided, if the fruits of his
royal favour were not often stopped in other hands. But your
Lordship has given me occasion not to complain of courts
whilst you are there. I have found the effects of your
mediation in all my concernments; and they were so much 80
the more noble in you because they were wholly voluntary. I
became your Lordship's (if I may venture on the similitude)
as the world was made, without knowing him who made it;
and brought only a passive obedience to be your creature.
This nobleness of yours I think myself the rather obliged to 85
own, because otherwise it must have been lost to all remembrance, for you are endued with that excellent quality of a
frank nature, to forget the good which you have done.

But, my Lord, I ought to have considered that you are as
great a judge as you are a patron; and that in praising you ill 90
I shall incur a higher note of ingratitude than that I thought to
have avoided. I stand in need of all your accustomed goodness
for the Dedication of this play, which though, perhaps, it be
the best of my comedies, is yet so faulty that I should have
feared you for my critic if I had not with some policy given 95
you the trouble of being my protector. Wit seems to have

---

67 *censures.* Q2 (censures Q1)

64–5 *least...men* Rochester defends in others whatever trace there may be of the wit he
    has himself in abundance.
82 *if I may venture* Dryden's flattery reaches an almost preposterous level of emphasis,
    but then often when Dryden seizes on a rhetorical idea, he pursues it simply as a
    shape, without regard to anything more atmospheric. Rochester 'created' Dryden
    in the way that God created the world, without the world knowing who its creator
    was. See also p. xviii.
95 *policy* tactical forethought

lodged itself more nobly in this age than in any of the former, and people of my mean condition are only writers because some of the nobility, and your Lordship in the first place, are above the narrow praises which poesie could give you. But let those who love to see themselves exceeded encourage your Lordship in so dangerous a quality: for my own part, I must confess that I have so much of self interest, as to be content with reading some papers of your verses, without desiring you should proceed to a scene or play: with the common prudence of those who are worsted in a duel, and declare they are satisfied when they are first wounded. Your Lordship has but another step to make, and from the patron of wit you may become its tyrant, and oppress our little reputations with more ease than you now protect them. But these, my Lord, are designs which I am sure you harbour not, any more than the French king is contriving the conquest of the Swissers. 'Tis a barren triumph, which is not worth your pains, and would only rank him amongst your slaves, who is already,

   My Lord,
    Your Lordship's
     Most obedient and most faithful servant,
     JOHN DRYDEN.

100

105

110

97 *more...age* This seems to mean 'wit is more the province of the nobility', but also perhaps 'is held in higher esteem'. It was Dryden's constant opinion, and that of his contemporaries, that Restoration society was wittier and more sophisticated than what it had replaced, and that for this the king and his court were chiefly responsible.

112 *Swissers* The Swiss cantons were at this time, as ever, politically too insignificant for Louis XIV to bother with.

PROLOGUE

Lord, how reformed and quiet we are grown,
Since all our braves and all our wits are gone:
Fop-corner now is free from civil war:
White-wig and vizard make no longer jar.
France, and the fleet, have swept the town so clear,   5
That we can act in peace, and you can hear.
'Twas a sad sight, before they marched from home,
To see our warriors in red waistcoats come,
With hair tucked up, into our tiring-room.
But 'twas more sad to hear their last adieu,   10
The women sobbed, and swore they would be true;
And so they were, as long as e'er they could:
But powerful guinea cannot be withstood,
And they were made of playhouse flesh and blood.
Fate did their friends for double use ordain,   15
In wars abroad they grinning honour gain,
And mistresses, for all that stay, maintain.
Now they are gone, 'tis dead vacation here,
For neither friends nor enemies appear.
Poor pensive punk now peeps ere plays begin,   20

The Prologue (with slight textual differences) was published the year before *Marriage A-la-Mode* was printed, in *Covent Garden Drolery*, and it was there said to have been spoken by Charles Hart (c. 1630–83), who created the part of Palamede.

2 *Since...gone* Preparations for the Third Dutch War, which would certainly have involved part of the usual theatre audience, were in hand some months before the war was actually declared, on 17 March 1672. The war had been agreed upon in a secret treaty with France on 22 May 1670. See note at IV. iv. 123–6.

3 *Fop-corner* This was a corner of the pit at the front where the fops gathered in their powdered wigs (White-wig), to engage in the battle of the sexes (civil war) with masked prostitutes (vizard).

9 *tucked up* The hair was tied back in a queue as part of military dress.

16 *grinning honour* glorious death in battle. The reference is to Falstaff in *1 Henry IV*: 'I like not such grinning honour as Sir Walter hath' (V. iii). The dead heroes ensure there are mistresses available for those who stayed behind and are alive.

18 *dead vacation* The audience is so depleted that it's like the four times a year when the law courts do not sit and keep people in town.

20 *Poor pensive punk* The charge for admission to the pit was half a crown. The punk (= prostitute) decides there are not enough potential customers (usually also at half a crown a time) to justify the expenditure, and tries her fortune instead in the Mall, the street bordering the northern side of St James's Park, a good place for trade. See Epilogue 20.

Sees the bare bench, and dares not venture in:
But manages her last half-crown with care,
And trudges to the Mall, on foot, for air.
Our city friends so far will hardly come,
They can take up with pleasures nearer home;   25
And see gay shows and gawdy scenes elsewhere:
For we presume they seldom come to hear.
But they have now ta'en up a glorious trade,
And cutting Moorcraft struts in masquerade.
There's all our hope, for we shall show today,   30
A masquing ball, to recommend our play:
Nay, to endear them more, and let them see,
We scorn to come behind in courtesy,
We'll follow the new mode which they begin,
And treat them with a room, and couch within: 35
For that's one way, howe'er the play fall short,
To oblige the town, the city, and the court.

24 *city friends* This is a scornful reference by the King's Company to the city audience
   of the splendid new Dorset Garden Theatre (owned by the Duke's Company and
   opened on 9 November 1671), which was very conveniently situated for the city.
   The King's Company moved from the Theatre Royal in Bridges Street, off Drury
   Lane, after its destruction by fire on 25 February 1672, to the Duke's old theatre in
   Lincoln's Inn Fields, which was itself more convenient for the city. This may
   suggest a first performance of *Marriage A-la-Mode* before the fire moved the King's
   Company nearer to a city audience. See pp. xii–xiii and notes at Dedication 2, I.i. 182
   and IV. iii. 190.
29 *cutting...masquerade* Moorcraft is the usurer turned gallant in Beaumont and
   Fletcher's play *The Scornful Lady* (1616). The allusion here is to an ordinary citizen
   who changes his usual trade for the 'glorious trade' of being a swaggering ('cutting')
   man about town. Masquerades were very popular and much satirised at this time
   for the freedom and sexual licence they encouraged. The link with the theatre and
   its play-acting was plain; and there is a masquerade at court in IV. ii of *Marriage
   A-la-Mode*, as the next lines of the prologue promise. The 'room, and couch' (line
   35) which are promised but do not actually materialise (at V. i. 210) make explicit
   the sexual interest of the masquerade, and the song with which the play now
   immediately begins releases the audience into an atmosphere of sexual freedom
   which the theatre powerfully offers, 'howe'er the play fall short' (line 36). See
   IV. iii. 128–34, IV. i. 134–44 and note.

PERSONS REPRESENTED

MEN

	By
Polydamas, Usurper of Sicily	Mr WINTERSHALL
Leonidas, the Rightful Prince, unknown	Mr KYNASTON
Argaleon, Favourite to Polydamas	Mr LYDALL
Hermogenes, Foster-father to Leonidas	Mr CARTWRIGHT
Eubulus, his Friend and Companion	Mr WATSON
Rhodophil, Captain of the Guards	Mr MOHUN
Palamede, a Courtier	Mr HART

WOMEN

	By
Palmyra, Daughter to the Usurper	Mrs COXE
Amalthea, Sister to Argaleon	Mrs JAMES
Doralice, Wife to Rhodophil	Mrs MARSHALL
Melantha, an Affected Lady	Mrs BOWTELL
Philotis, Woman to Melantha	Mrs REEVE
Beliza, Woman to Doralice	Mrs SLADE
Artemis, a Court Lady	Mrs UPHILL

[Straton, Messenger, Ladies, Gentlemen, Citizens, Attendants, Guards, Servants, Torchbearers]

Scene, SICILY

Beliza D (Belisa Q1)

9

MARRIAGE A-LA MODE

Act I, Scene i

Walks near the court
Enter DORALICE *and* BELIZA

DORALICE
Beliza, bring the lute into this arbour, the walks are empty:
I would try the song the Princess Amalthea bade me
learn.

They go in, and sing

1.

Why should a foolish marriage vow
   Which long ago was made,   5
Oblige us to each other now
   When passion is decayed?
We loved and we loved, as long as we could,
   Till our love was loved out in us both:
But our marriage is dead, when the pleasure is fled: 10
   'Twas pleasure first made it an oath.

2.

If I have pleasures for a friend,
   And farther love in store,
What wrong has he whose joys did end,
   And who could give no more?   15
'Tis a madness that he, should be jealous of me,
   Or that I should bar him of another:
For all we can gain, is to give ourselves pain,
   When neither can hinder the other.

Enter PALAMEDE *in riding habit, and hears the song*
Re-enter DORALICE *and* BELIZA

16, 18 *These lines are each printed in couplets in Q1, and what are consequently the last six
lines of the song are indented equally to match the first line of the stanza.*

---

1 *walks* avenues, perhaps set with trees
4 *Why should...* The song was set to music by Robert Smith (?–1675), who composed
a great deal for the theatre, and particularly for the Dorset Garden Theatre. A
striking song here, unusually not in triple time but common time, and by a
composer much associated with the Duke's Company, seems intended to lure a city
audience, as the last lines of the prologue rather equivocally promise.

BELIZA
    Madam, a stranger.   20

DORALICE
    I did not think to have had witnesses of my bad singing.

PALAMEDE
    If I have erred, Madam, I hope you'll pardon the curiosity of
    a stranger; for I may well call myself so, after five years'
    absence from the court. But you have freed me from one error.

DORALICE
    What's that, I beseech you?   25

PALAMEDE
    I thought good voices and ill faces had been inseparable;
    and that to be fair and sing well had been only the privilege
    of angels.

DORALICE
    And how many more of these fine things can you say to me?

PALAMEDE
    Very few, Madam, for if I should continue to see you some   30
    hours longer: you look so killingly that I should be mute
    with wonder.

DORALICE
    This will not give you the reputation of a wit with me. You
    travelling monsieurs live upon the stock you have got
    abroad for the first day or two: to repeat with a good   35
    memory, and apply with a good grace is all your wit. And
    commonly your gullets are sewed up, like cormorants.
    When you have regorged what you have taken in, you are
    the leanest things in nature.

PALAMEDE
    Then, Madam, I think you had best make that use of me.   40
    Let me wait on you for two or three days together, and you
    shall hear all I have learnt of extraordinary in other
    countries. And one thing which I never saw till I came home,
    that is, a lady of a better voice, better face, and better wit
    than any I have seen abroad. And after this, if I should not   45
    declare myself most passionately in love with you, I should
    have less wit than yet you think I have.

DORALICE
    A very plain and pithy declaration. I see, Sir, you have been
    travelling in Spain or Italy, or some of the hot countries,

31 *killingly* stunning. There may just be some other resonance here as well; see note
    at IV. iii. 111.
37 *cormorants* a large and proverbially greedy seabird used for catching fish. A cord
    was tied round the bird's neck to prevent it swallowing the fish it caught.
42 *of extraordinary* that is extraordinary

where men come to the point immediately. But are you sure   50
these are not words of course? For I would not give my
poor heart an occasion of complaint against me, that I
engaged it too rashly, and then could not bring it off.

PALAMEDE

Your heart may trust itself with me safely; I shall use it
very civilly while it stays, and never turn it away without   55
fair warning to provide for itself.

DORALICE

First, then, I do receive your passion with as little consideration on my part as ever you gave it me on yours. And
now see what a miserable wretch you have made yourself.

PALAMEDE

Who, I miserable? Thank you for that. Give me love   60
enough, and life enough, and I defy fortune.

DORALICE

Know then, thou man of vain imagination, know to thy
utter confusion, that I am virtuous.

PALAMEDE

Such another word, and I give up the ghost.

DORALICE

Then, to strike you quite dead, know that I am married too.   65

PALAMEDE

Art thou married; O thou damnable virtuous woman?

DORALICE

Yes, married to a gentleman; young, handsome, rich,
valiant, and with all the good qualities that will make you
despair, and hang yourself.

PALAMEDE

Well, in spite of all that, I'll love you. Fortune has cut us   70
out for one another, for I am to be married within these
three days. Married past redemption, to a young, fair,

---

51 *of course* of a usual conversational sort

57–8 *consideration* deliberation

62 *thou…imagination* There is a distinct mock-serious Scriptural note here. Compare
perhaps Romans 1:21.

66 *Art…woman?* The punctuation, which I have left unemended instead of replacing
the semi-colon with a comma, indicates how the apostrophe 'O thou damnable virtuous woman' is hovering on the edge of freeing itself from its entangling syntax.
No doubt the actor on the stage gave it all he could as a mock-serious moment of
high rant; and gradually the printed text followed suit. Already by Q2 the question
mark had been replaced by an exclamation mark (producing rather an odd inter-
mediate state of punctuation); and in Q4 the semi-colon in addition gave way to a
question mark and freed the ranting moment entirely.

rich, and virtuous lady. And it shall go hard but I will love
my wife as little as I perceive you do your husband.

DORALICE

Remember, I invade no propriety. My servant you are   75
only till you are married.

PALAMEDE

In the mean time, you are to forget you have a husband.

DORALICE

And you, that you are to have a wife.

BELIZA (*aside to her lady*)

O Madam, my lord's just at the end of the walks; and, if
you make not haste, will discover you.   80

DORALICE

Some other time, new servant, we'll talk further of the
premisses. In the mean while, break not my first command-
ment, that is, not to follow me.

PALAMEDE

But where, then, shall I find you again?

DORALICE

At court. Yours for two days, Sir.   85

PALAMEDE

And nights, I beseech you, Madam.

Exit DORALICE *and* BELIZA

PALAMEDE

Well, I'll say that for thee, thou art a very dextrous
executioner; thou hast done my business at one stroke.
Yet I must marry another – and yet I must love this;
and if it lead me into some little inconveniences, as   90
jealousies, and duels, and death, and so forth; yet while
sweet love is in the case, Fortune do thy worst, and avaunt
Mortality.

Enter RHODOPHIL, *who seems speaking to one within*

RHODOPHIL

Leave them with my lieutenant, while I fetch new orders

---

73 *it...but* it can hardly be doubted that
75 *no propriety* no one else's proper sphere
82 *premisses* the matters just spoken about. Possibly the word is used with some sense
that it can also mean specified buildings and grounds, so that there is the hint that
Doralice will appoint a place of assignation, as in fact she does (again by indirection)
at II. i. 233–6.
92–3 *avaunt Mortality* This looks as though it should mean something like 'away with
human frailty!' but I think in fact it means 'onward humanity!' (in defiance of
fortune). As an interjection, 'avaunt' (from French 'avant') can mean both
'forward!' and 'be off, begone!'

from the king. (*sees* PALAMEDE) How? Palamede!   95

PALAMEDE
Rhodophil!

RHODOPHIL
Who thought to have seen you in Sicily?

PALAMEDE
Who thought to have found the court so far from Syracuse?

RHODOPHIL
The king best knows the reason of the progress. But answer
me, I beseech you, what brought you home from travel?   100

PALAMEDE
The commands of an old rich father.

RHODOPHIL
And the hopes of burying him?

PALAMEDE
Both together, as you see, have prevailed on my good
nature. In few words: my old man has already married me;
for he has agreed with another old man, as rich and as   105
covetous as himself; the articles are drawn, and I have
given my consent, for fear of being disinherited; and yet
know not what kind of woman I am to marry.

RHODOPHIL
Sure your father intends you some very ugly wife; and has
a mind to keep you in ignorance, till you have shot the gulf.   110

PALAMEDE
I know not that; but obey I will, and must.

RHODOPHIL
Then I cannot choose but grieve for all the good girls and
courtesans of France and Italy. They have lost the most
kind-hearted, doting, prodigal, humble servant in Europe.

PALAMEDE
All I could do in these three years I stayed behind you, was   115
to comfort the poor creatures for the loss of you. But what's
the reason that in all this time, a friend could never hear
from you?

RHODOPHIL
Alas, dear Palamede, I have had no joy to write, nor indeed
to do anything in the world to please me. The greatest   120
misfortune imaginable is fallen upon me.

PALAMEDE
Prithee, what's the matter?

---

98 *Syracuse* a town on the east coast of Sicily
110 *shot the gulf* There is not so much a sense here of a daring enterprise completed as of
an irrevocable passage from one state to another.

RHODOPHIL
  In one word, I am married; wretchedly married; and have
  been above these two years. Yes, faith, the devil has had power
  over me, in spite of my vows and resolutions to the contrary. 125
PALAMEDE
  I find you have sold yourself for filthy lucre; she's old, or
  ill-conditioned.
RHODOPHIL
  No, none of these. I'm sure she's young; and, for her
  humour, she laughs, sings, and dances eternally; and, which
  is more, we never quarrel about it, for I do the same.   130
PALAMEDE
  You're very unfortunate indeed. Then the case is plain, she
  is not handsome.
RHODOPHIL
  A great beauty too, as people say.
PALAMEDE
  As people say? Why, you should know that best yourself.
RHODOPHIL
  Ask those who have smelt to a strong perfume two years   135
  together, what's the scent.
PALAMEDE
  But here are good qualities enough for one woman.
RHODOPHIL
  Ay, too many, Palamede. If I could put them into three or
  four women, I should be content.
PALAMEDE
  O, now I have found it. You dislike her for no other reason   140
  but because she's your wife.
RHODOPHIL
  And is not that enough? All that I know of her perfections now
  is only by memory. I remember, indeed, that about two years
  ago I loved her passionately; but those golden days are gone,
  Palamede. Yet I loved her a whole half year, double the natural 145
  term of any mistress, and think in my conscience I could
  have held out another quarter; but then the world began to
  laugh at me, and a certain shame of being out of fashion seized
  me. At last we arrived at that point, that there was nothing
  left in us to make us new to one another. Yet still I set a good 150
  face upon the matter, and am infinite fond of her before
  company; but when we are alone, we walk like lions in a
  room, she one way, and I another. And we lie with our backs

148 *out of fashion* for loving a mistress so long

to each other so far distant, as if the fashion of great beds was
only invented to keep husband and wife sufficiently asunder. 155
PALAMEDE
The truth is, your disease is very desperate. But though you
cannot be cured, you may be patched up a little. You must
get you a mistress, Rhodophil: that, indeed, is living upon
cordials; but as fast as one fails, you must supply it with
another. You're like a gamester who has lost his estate; yet 160
in doing that you have learnt the advantages of play, and
can arrive to live upon't.
RHODOPHIL
Truth is, I have been thinking on't, and have just resolved
to take your counsel; and faith, considering the damned
disadvantages of a married man, I have provided well 165
enough, for a poor humble sinner, that is not ambitious of
great matters.
PALAMEDE
What is she, for a woman?
RHODOPHIL
One of the stars of Syracuse, I assure you. Young enough,
fair enough, and, but for one quality, just such a woman as 170
I would wish.
PALAMEDE
O friend, this is not an age to be critical in beauty. When
we had good store of handsome women, and but few chap-
men, you might have been more curious in your choice.
But now the price is enhanced upon us, and all mankind 175
set up for mistresses, so that poor little creatures, without
beauty, birth, or breeding, but only impudence, go off at
unreasonable rates; and a man, in these hard times, snaps
at them, as he does at broad-gold, never examines the
weight, but takes light or heavy as he can get it. 180
RHODOPHIL
But my mistress has one fault that's almost unpardonable.

154 *fashion...beds* The Restoration introduced a revolution in English furniture,
walnut, for instance, replacing oak as the favoured wood. The great or State beds of
the Restoration were large, richly draped and quite unlike the carved wooden beds
of the Elizabethan and Jacobean period.
159 *cordials* invigorating medicines, but of very temporary effect
173–4 *chapman* men engaged in the business of buying and selling; here, men in the
market for women
179 *broad-gold* the good old money. The old twenty shilling gold pieces, which were
larger than the gold guinea introduced in 1663, were consequently known as broad
pieces or broad gold. Many of these old coins were lighter than their proclaimed
weight because they had been illegally clipped over the years.

For, being a town-lady, without any relation to the court,
yet she thinks herself undone if she be not seen there three
or four times a day, with the Princess Amalthea. And for
the king, she haunts and watches him so narrowly in a   185
morning, that she prevents even the chemists who beset
his chamber, to turn their mercury into his gold.
PALAMEDE
Yet hitherto, methinks, you are no very unhappy man.
RHODOPHIL
With all this, she's the greatest gossip in nature; for,
besides the court, she's the most eternal visitor of the town: 190
and yet manages her time so well, that she seems ubiquitary.
For my part, I can compare her to nothing but the sun, for,
like him, she takes no rest, nor ever sets in one place, but to
rise in another.
PALAMEDE
I confess she had need be handsome with these qualities.   195
RHODOPHIL
No lady can be so curious of a new fashion, as she is of a
new French word. She's the very mint of the nation; and
as fast as any bullion comes out of France, coins it
immediately into our language.
PALAMEDE
And her name is –   200
RHODOPHIL
No naming; that's not like a cavalier. Find her, if you can,
by my description; and I am not so ill a painter, that I need
write the name beneath the picture.
PALAMEDE
Well, then, how far have you proceeded in your love?
RHODOPHIL
'Tis yet in the bud, and what fruit it may bear I cannot tell;   205
for this insufferable humour of haunting the court is so
predominant, that she has hitherto broken all her assig-
nations with me, for fear of missing her visits there.

182 *town-lady* This may be allegedly Sicily, but the terminology, of course, refers to
seventeenth-century London. The 'town' was the fashionable society of London,
though distinct from the court; the 'city', by contrast, was the less fashionable
business and commercial society of London, centred round the north side of London Bridge. See III. i. 156–66 for the complete social chain.
186 *prevents* arrives before
    chemists The alchemist was preoccupied with turning base metal into gold; these
    more modern chemists make gold by the more modern method of offering remedies
    for payment. Mercury was chiefly used as a cure for syphilis.
191 *ubiquitary* to be found in every place

PALAMEDE

That's the hardest part of your adventure. But, for aught I
see, fortune has used us both alike; I have a strange kind   210
of mistress too in court, besides her I am to marry.

RHODOPHIL

You have made haste to be in love then; for, if I am not
mistaken, you are but this day arrived.

PALAMEDE

That's all one, I have seen the lady already who has charmed
me, seen her in these walks, courted her, and received, for   215
the first time, an answer that does not put me into despair.

To them ARGALEON, AMALTHEA, ARTEMIS

I'll tell you at more leisure my adventures. The walks fill
apace, I see. Stay, is not that the young Lord Argaleon,
the king's favourite?

RHODOPHIL

Yes, and as proud as ever, as ambitious, and as revengeful.   220

PALAMEDE

How keeps he the king's favour with these qualities?

RHODOPHIL

Argaleon's father helped him to the crown: besides, he gilds
over all his vices to the king, and standing in the dark to
him, sees all his inclinations, interests and humours, which
he so times and soothes that, in effect, he reigns.   225

PALAMEDE

His sister Amalthea, who, I guess, stands by him, seems
not to be of his temper.

RHODOPHIL

O, she's all goodness and generosity.

ARGALEON

Rhodophil, the king expects you earnestly.

RHODOPHIL

'Tis done, my Lord, what he commanded: I only waited his   230
return from hunting. Shall I attend your Lordship to him?

ARGALEON

No; I go first another way.

Exit hastily

222–4 *gilds...him* Argaleon disguises from the king all the king's own vices, and flatters
the king in a way he is unaware of. The lines might otherwise mean that Argaleon
disguises his own vices and thus is only as visible in his true nature to the king as a
man would be who stood in the dark. I incline to the first meaning on the grounds
that 'gilding' seems the kind of disguise appropriate for kingly vices, something a
little more elaborate than common or garden concealment.

PALAMEDE
    He seems in haste, and discomposed.
AMALTHEA (*to* RHODOPHIL, *after a short whisper*)
    Your friend? Then he must needs be of much merit.
RHODOPHIL
    When he has kissed the king's hand, I know he'll beg the   235
    honour to kiss yours. Come, Palamede.
               Exeunt RHODOPHIL *and* PALAMEDE, *bowing to* AMALTHEA
ARTEMIS
    Madam, you tell me most surprising news.
AMALTHEA
    The fear of it, you see,
    Has discomposed my brother; but to me
    All that can bring my country good is welcome.   240
ARTEMIS
    It seems incredible, that this old king,
    Whom all the world thought childless,
    Should come to search the farthest parts of Sicily,
    In hope to find an heir.
AMALTHEA
    To lessen your astonishment, I will   245
    Unfold some private passages of state,
    Of which you yet are ignorant. Know first,
    That this Polydamas who reigns, unjustly
    Gained the crown.
ARTEMIS
    Somewhat of this I have confusedly heard.   250
AMALTHEA
    I'll tell you all in brief: Theagenes,
    Our last great king,
    Had, by his queen, one only son, an infant
    Of three years old, called after him Theagenes;
    The general, this Polydamas, then married: 255
    The public feasts for which were scarcely past,
    When a rebellion in the heart of Sicily
    Called out the king to arms.
ARTEMIS   Polydamas
    Had then a just excuse to stay behind.
AMALTHEA
    His temper was too warlike to accept it: 260
    He left his bride, and the new joys of marriage,
    And followed to the field. In short, they fought,
    The rebels were o'ercome; but in the fight
    The too bold king received a mortal wound.
    When he perceived his end approaching near,   265

He called the general, to whose care he left
His widow queen and orphan son; then died.

ARTEMIS
Then false Polydamas betrayed his trust?

AMALTHEA
He did; and with my father's help, for which
Heaven pardon him, so gained the soldiers' hearts,   270
That in few days he was saluted king:
And when his crimes had impudence enough
To bear the eye of day,
He marched his army back to Syracuse.
But see how heaven can punish wicked men   275
In granting their desires: the news was brought him
That day he was to enter it, that Eubulus,
Whom his dead master had left governor,
Was fled, and with him bore away the queen,
And royal orphan; but, what more amazed him,   280
His wife, now big with child, and much detesting
Her husband's practices, had willingly
Accompanied their flight.

ARTEMIS
How I admire her virtue!

AMALTHEA   What became
Of her, and them, since that, was never known;   285
Only, some few days since, a famous robber
Was taken with some jewels of vast price,
Which when they were delivered to the king
He knew had been his wife's; with these a letter,
Much torn and sullied, but which yet he knew   290
To be her writing.

ARTEMIS   Sure from hence he learned
He had a son.

AMALTHEA   It was not left so plain:
The paper only said, she died in childbed:
But when it should have mentioned son or daughter,
Just there it was torn off.

ARTEMIS   Madam, the king.   295

---

292 *He* Q2 (he Q1)

---

276 *In granting* even while granting, by granting
293 *The...childbed* If, as seems intended, the 'paper' is the 'letter' of line 289, then it is
odd that Polydamas' wife should have written to say she died in childbed.
Buckingham parodies this slip in *The Rehearsal*, where Tom Thimble's first wife
writes a song 'after she was dead' (III. i. 93–5).

To them POLYDAMAS, ARGALEON, *Guard, and attendants*

ARGALEON
   The robber, though thrice racked, confessed no more
   But that he took those jewels near this place.
POLYDAMAS
   But yet the circumstances strongly argue,
   That those, for whom I search, are not far off.
ARGALEON
   I cannot easily believe it.
ARTEMIS (*aside*)   No,   300
   You would not have it so.
POLYDAMAS
   Those I employed have, in the neighbouring hamlet,
   Amongst the fishers' cabins, made discovery
   Of some young persons, whose uncommon beauty,
   And graceful carriage, make it seem suspicious   305
   They are not what they seem: I therefore sent
   The captain of my guards, this morning early,
   With orders to secure and bring them to me.

Enter RHODOPHIL *and* PALAMEDE

   O here he is. Have you performed my will?
RHODOPHIL
   Sir, those whom you commanded me to bring,   310
   Are waiting in the walks.
POLYDAMAS   Conduct them hither.
RHODOPHIL
   First, give me leave
   To beg your notice of this gentleman.
POLYDAMAS
   He seems to merit it. His name and quality?
RHODOPHIL
   Palamede, son to Lord Cleodemus of Palermo,   315
   And new returned from travel.

PALAMEDE *approaches, and kneels to kiss the king's hand*

POLYDAMAS   You're welcome.
   I knew your father well, he was both brave
   And honest; we two once were fellow soldiers

---

317 *I...well* There is perhaps an echo of Bertram's first meeting with the king in *All's Well That Ends Well* I. ii.

In the last civil wars.

PALAMEDE

I bring the same unquestioned honesty   320
And zeal to serve your Majesty; the courage
You were pleased to praise in him,
Your royal prudence, and your people's love,
Will never give me leave to try like him
In civil wars. I hope it may in foreign.   325

POLYDAMAS

Attend the court, and it shall be my care
To find out some employment worthy you.
Go, Rhodophil, and bring in those without.

Exeunt RHODOPHIL *and* PALAMEDE

RHODOPHIL *returns again immediately, and with him
enter* HERMOGENES, LEONIDAS *and* PALMYRA

Behold two miracles! (*looking earnestly on* LEONIDAS *and*
                                        PALMYRA)

Of different sexes, but of equal form: 330
So matchless both, that my divided soul
Can scarcely ask the gods a son or daughter,
For fear of losing one. If from your hands,
You powers, I shall this day receive a daughter,
Argaleon, she is yours; but if a son,   335
Then Amalthea's love shall make him happy.

ARGALEON

Grant, heaven, this admirable nymph may prove
That issue which he seeks.

AMALTHEA

Venus Urania, if thou art a goddess,
Grant that sweet youth may prove the prince of Sicily.   340

POLYDAMAS (*to* HERMOGENES)

Tell me, old man, and tell me true, from whence
Had you that youth and maid?

319 *civil wars* It is difficult to know to what civil wars Polydamas refers, since he
usurped the crown without bloodshed, as we have just heard. He may perhaps refer
outside the play to the civil wars in England. Why, too, does he not know Palamede,
who has only been away from the court for five years (I.i.23–4)? Palamede is
perhaps a shadowy Argaleon-like figure here: he has a father, as did Argaleon
(I.i.222), who served Polydamas well; and he swears loyalty to Polydamas as a good
king (I.i.320–5), thus unintentionally gilding over his vices in a way that is particularly ironic in view of what we have just heard about Polydamas' treachery.
Argaleon, then, is the knowing courtier, who acquiesces readily in the evil of the
situation; Palamede the innocent, who assumes the king is what he seems.

339 *Venus Urania* Celestial Venus, the goddess of love

HERMOGENES   From whence you had
   Your sceptre, Sir: I had them from the gods.
POLYDAMAS
   The gods then have not such another gift.
   Say who their parents were.
HERMOGENES   My wife, and I.   345
ARGALEON
   It is not likely,
   A virgin of so excellent a beauty
   Should come from such a stock.
AMALTHEA
   Much less, that such a youth, so sweet, so graceful,
   Should be produced from peasants.   350
HERMOGENES
   Why, nature is the same in villages,
   And much more fit to form a noble issue
   Where it is least corrupted.
POLYDAMAS
   He talks too like a man that knew the world
   To have been long a peasant. But the rack   355
   Will teach him other language. Hence with him.

   As the Guard are carrying him away, his peruke falls off

   Sure I have seen that face before. Hermogenes!
   'Tis he, 'tis he who fled away with Eubulus,
   And with my dear Eudocia.
HERMOGENES
   Yes, Sir, I am Hermogenes.   360
   And if to have been loyal be a crime,
   I stand prepared to suffer.
POLYDAMAS
   If thou would'st live, speak quickly.
   What is become of my Eudocia?

---

345 *I.* Q1a (I Q1)
359 *Eudocia* ed. (*Eudoxia* Q1)
364 *Eudocia* ed. (*Eudoxia* Q1)

356+ *peruke falls off* This must have been a much enjoyed dramatic moment.
Buckingham seems to parody it in *The Rehearsal*, where Bayes' peruke falls off as he
scratches his head (IV. ii. 67+). There is oddity of more than one kind here: it seems
strange that a peasant should have been wearing a peruke in the first place; and
strange too that it should so effectively have disguised Hermogenes. The peruke as
an effective disguise appears again at IV. iii. 72+.

Where is the queen and young Theagenes?   365
Where Eubulus? And which of these is mine? (*pointing to*
                LEONIDAS *and* PALMYRA)
HERMOGENES
  Eudocia is dead, so is the queen,
  The infant king her son, and Eubulus.
POLYDAMAS
  Traitor, 'tis false: produce them, or –
HERMOGENES   Once more
  I tell you, they are dead; but leave to threaten,   370
  For you shall know no further.
POLYDAMAS
  Then prove indulgent to my hopes, and be
  My friend for ever. Tell me, good Hermogenes,
  Whose son is that brave youth?
HERMOGENES   Sir, he is yours.
POLYDAMAS
  Fool that I am, thou seest that so I wish it,   375
  And so thou flatterest me.
HERMOGENES   By all that's holy.
POLYDAMAS
  Again. Thou canst not swear too deeply.
  Yet hold, I will believe thee: – yet I doubt.
HERMOGENES
  You need not, Sir.
ARGALEON
  Believe him not; he sees you credulous,   380
  And would impose his own base issue on you,
  And fix it to your crown.
AMALTHEA
  Behold his goodly shape and feature, Sir;
  Methinks he much resembles you.
ARGALEON
  I say, if you have any issue here,   385
  It must be that fair creature;
  By all my hopes I think so.
AMALTHEA
  Yes, brother, I believe you by your hopes,
  For they are all for her.
POLYDAMAS   Call the youth nearer.

---

367 *Eudocia* ed. (*Eudoxia* Q1)
    queen, Q3 (Queen. Q1)

370 *leave* cease

HERMOGENES
> Leonidas, the king would speak with you.   390
POLYDAMAS
> Come near, and be not dazzled with the splendour
> And greatness of a court.
LEONIDAS
> I need not this encouragement.
> I can fear nothing but the gods.
> And for this glory, after I have seen   395
> The canopy of state spread wide above
> In the abyss of heaven, the court of stars,
> The blushing morning, and the rising sun,
> What greater can I see?
POLYDAMAS (*embracing him*)
> This speaks thee born a prince, thou art thyself   400
> That rising sun, and shalt not see on earth
> A brighter than thy self. – All of you witness,
> That for my son I here receive this youth,
> This brave, this – but I must not praise him further,
> Because he now is mine.   405
LEONIDAS (*kneeling*)
> I would not, Sir, believe
> That I am made your sport;
> For I find nothing in myself, but what
> Is much above a scorn; I dare give credit
> To whatso'er a king, like you, can tell me.   410
> Either I am, or will deserve to be your son.
ARGALEON
> I yet maintain it is impossible
> This young man should be yours; for, if he were,
> Why should Hermógenes so long conceal him
> When he might gain so much by his discovery?   415
HERMOGENES (*to the king*)
> I stayed a while to make him worthy, Sir, of you.
> But in that time I found
> Somewhat within him which so moved my love,
> I never could resolve to part with him.
LEONIDAS (*to* ARGALEON)
> You ask too many questions, and are   420
> Too saucy for a subject.
ARGALEON
> You rather over-act your part, and are
> Too soon a prince.
LEONIDAS   Too soon you'll find me one.

POLYDAMAS
  Enough, Argaleon;
  I have declared him mine: and you, Leonidas,   425
  Live well with him I love.
ARGALEON
  Sir, if he be your son, I may have leave
  To think your queen had twins; look on this virgin;
  Hermogenes would enviously deprive you
  Of half your treasure.
HERMOGENES   Sir, she is my daughter.   430
  I could, perhaps, thus aided by this lord,
  Prefer her to be yours; but truth forbid
  I should procure her greatness by a lie.
POLYDAMAS
  Come hither, beauteous maid: are you not sorry
  Your father will not let you pass for mine?   435
PALMYRA
  I am content to be what heaven has made me.
POLYDAMAS
  Could you not wish yourself a princess then?
PALMYRA
  Not to be sister to Leonidas.
POLYDAMAS
  Why, my sweet maid?
PALMYRA   Indeed I cannot tell;
  But I could be content to be his handmaid.   440
ARGALEON (aside)
  I wish I had not seen her.
PALMYRA (to LEONIDAS)
  I must weep for your good fortune;
  Pray pardon me, indeed I cannot help it.
  Leonidas (alas, I had forgot,
  Now I must call you prince) but must I leave you?   445
LEONIDAS (aside)
  I dare not speak to her; for if I should,
  I must weep too.
POLYDAMAS
  No, you shall live at court, sweet Innocence,
  And see him there. Hermogenes,
  Though you intended not to make me happy,   450
  Yet you shall be rewarded for the event.
  Come, my Leonidas, let's thank the gods;

---

438 Not...Leonidas In All's Well That Ends Well I. iii Helena for a similar reason does
  not want to be Bertram's sister.

Thou for a father, I for such a son.

Exeunt all but LEONIDAS and PALMYRA

LEONIDAS

My dear Palmyra, many eyes observe me,
And I have thoughts so tender, that I cannot   455
In public speak them to you: some hours hence
I shall shake off these crowds of fawning courtiers,
And then –

Exit LEONIDAS

PALMYRA

Fly swift, you hours, you measure time for me in vain,
Till you bring back Leonidas again.   460
Be shorter now; and to redeem that wrong,
When he and I are met, be twice as long.

Exit

Act II, Scene i

MELANTHA *and* PHILOTIS

PHILOTIS

Count Rhodophil's a fine gentleman indeed, Madam; and I
think deserves your affection.

MELANTHA

Let me die but he's a fine man; he sings, and dances *en
français*, and writes the *billets doux* to a miracle.

PHILOTIS

And those are no small talents, to a lady that understands   5
and values the French air, as your Ladyship does.

MELANTHA

How charming is the French air! And what an *étourdie bête*
is one of our untravelled islanders! When he would make
his court to me, let me die but he is just Aesop's ass, that
would imitate the courtly French in his addresses; but,   10
instead of those, comes pawing upon me, and doing all
things so *maladroitly*.

---

3 *Let me die but* I swear that
4 *billets doux* love notes
6 *air* manner
7 *étourdie bête* senseless beast
9 *Aesop's ass* a byword for laughable foolishness
12 *maladroitly* clumsily

PHILOTIS
    'Tis great pity Rhodophil's a married man, that you may
    not have an honourable intrigue with him.

MELANTHA
    Intrigue, Philotis! That's an old phrase; I have laid that   15
    word by. *Amour* sounds better. But thou art heir to all my
    cast words, as thou art to my old wardrobe. Oh Count
    Rhodophil! Ah *mon cher!* I could live and die with him.

               Enter PALAMEDE *and a* SERVANT

SERVANT
    Sir, this is my Lady.   [*Exit* SERVANT]

PALAMEDE
    Then this is she that is to be divine, and nymph, and god-   20
    dess, and with whom I am to be desperately in love. (*bows to
    her, delivering a letter*) This letter, Madam, which I present
    you from your father, has given me both the happy oppor-
    tunity, and the boldness, to kiss the fairest hands in Sicily.

MELANTHA
    Came you lately from Palermo, Sir?   25

PALAMEDE
    But yesterday, Madam.

MELANTHA (*reading the letter*)
    *Daughter, receive the bearer of this letter, as a gentleman whom
    I have chosen to make you happy;* [*aside*] (O Venus, a new
    servant sent me! And let me die but he has the air of a *galant
    homme*) *his father is the rich Lord Cleodemus, our neighbour: I*   30
    *suppose you'll find nothing disagreeable in his person or his con-
    verse, both which he has improved by travel. The treaty is already
    concluded, and I shall be in town within these three days; so
    that you have nothing to do, but to obey your careful father.*
    (*to* PALAMEDE) Sir, my father, for whom I have a blind   35
    obedience, has commanded me to receive your passionate

---

29 *galant* (gallant Q1. *The reading of* Q1 *makes perfectly good sense, but there seems little
    point in having only half of a standard term in French, so I suppose this is a compositor's
    error.*)

---

14 *intrigue* This is itself a French loan-word, and perfectly current in the sense of an
    affair or liaison between a man and a woman; but Melantha demands greater novelty
    in her borrowing from French. A French word become current English interests
    her little, unless perhaps she can frenchify it again.
25 *Palermo* a town on the north coast of Sicily

addresses; but you must also give me leave to avow that I
cannot merit them, from so accomplished a cavalier.

PALAMEDE

I want many things, Madam, to render me accomplished;
and the first and greatest of them is your favour.   40

MELANTHA

Let me die, Philotis, but this is extremely French; but yet
Count Rhodophil – [*to* PALAMEDE] A gentleman, Sir, that
understands the *grand monde* so well, who has haunted the
best *conversations*, and who (in short) has *voyaged*, may
pretend to the *good graces* of any lady.   45

PALAMEDE (*aside*)

Hey day! *grand monde! conversation! voyaged!* and *good
graces!* I find my mistress is one of those that run mad in
new French words.

MELANTHA

I suppose, Sir, you have made the *tour* of France; and
having seen all that's *fine* there, will make a considerable   50
réformation in the rudeness of our court: for let me die but
an unfashioned, untravelled, mere Sicilian is a *bête;* and
has nothing in the world of an *honnête homme*.

PALAMEDE

I must confess, Madam, that –

MELANTHA

And what new *menuets* have you brought over with you?   55
Their *menuets* are to a miracle! And our Sicilian jigs are so

---

43–5 *conversations...voyaged...good graces* (*These words are left unitalicised in* Q1, *but
Palamede's reaction to them makes clear that Melantha speaks them in a self-consciously
French way.*)

50 *fine* (fine Q1. *See textual note at II. i. 66.*)

51 *reformation* (reformation Q1)

55 *you?* F (you! Q1)

56 *jigs* F (*Jigs* Q1)

---

43 *grand monde* great world, the world of sophistication and refined manners
haunted been assiduously present at. This seems to be not an affected use; it is only
more recently that the sense of the word has been chiefly ghostly.

46–7 *grand...graces* Palamede's selection of frenchified elements in Melantha's
speech comprises words clearly French and words that could be self-consciously
pronounced so as to make them acknowledge again their French origins. Melantha
explores both possibilities in her speech, though chiefly the first. I imagine that the
one plainly Anglo-Saxon word in the selection here, 'good', was dragged across the
Channel in the wake of 'graces'

51 *rudeness* lack of sophistication

53 *honnête homme* gentleman

55 *menuets* minuets

dull and *fade* to them!

PALAMEDE

For *menuets*, Madam –

MELANTHA

And what new plays are there in *vogue?* And who danced
best in the last *grand ballet?* Come, sweet servant, you shall   60
tell me all.

PALAMEDE (*aside*)

Tell her all? Why, she asks all, and will hear nothing – To
answer in order, Madam, to your demands –

MELANTHA

I am thinking what a happy couple we shall be! For you
shall keep up your *correspondance* abroad, and everything   65
that's new writ in France, and *fine*, I mean all that's
delicate, and *bien tourné*, we will have first.

PALAMEDE

But, Madam, our fortune –

MELANTHA

I understand you, Sir; you'll leave that to me. For the
ménage of a family, I know it better than any lady in Sicily.   70

PALAMEDE

Alas, Madam, we –

MELANTHA

Then, we will never make visits together, nor see a play, but
always apart. You shall be every day at the king's *levée*, and I
at the queen's; and we will never meet but in the drawing-room.

---

57 *fade* ed. (fad Q1. *The compositor of Q2 was clearly puzzled by the* Q1 *reading and turned
it into comprehensible English as* sad, *assuming* f *had been set by mistake for long* s. Q3,
Q4, F, D *follow suit.*)

59 *vogue* (vogue Q1)

60 *grand ballet* (Grand Ballet Q1)

65 *correspondance* (correspondence Q1)

66 *fine* (fine Q1. *Melantha immediately glosses the word to make clear her use of the French
sense.*)

70 *ménage* mennage Q1)

---

57 *fade* insipid

67 *bien tourné* well expressed, elegant

70 *ménage* household management

73 *levée* rising from bed

74 *queen's* This is odd because Polydamas' queen is dead. Melantha is perhaps in an
ideal world here, though it seems more likely that this is Dryden's slip, because
Melantha has habitually an enthusiasm for royalty which is simultaneously idealis-
ing and acutely aware of the actual day-to-day state of things in the court, who's in
who's out.

PHILOTIS
Madam, the new prince is just passed by the end of the walk.   75
MELANTHA
The new prince, sayest thou? Adieu, dear servant; I have not
made my court to him these two long hours. O, 'tis the
sweetest prince! So *obligeant, charmant, ravissant*, that –
Well, I'll make haste to kiss his hands; and then make half
a score visits more, and be with you again in a twinkling.   80
                              Exit, running, with PHILOTIS
PALAMEDE (*solus*)
Now heaven, of thy mercy, bless me from this tongue; it
may keep the field against a whole army of lawyers, and
that in their own language, French gibberish. 'Tis true, in
the day-time 'tis tolerable, when a man has field-room to
run from it. But to be shut up in a bed with her, like two   85
cocks in a pit; humanity cannot support it. I must kiss all
night, in my own defence, and hold her down, like a boy
at cuffs; nay, and give her the rising blow every time she
begins to speak.

                         Enter RHODOPHIL

But here comes Rhodophil. 'Tis pretty odd that my mistress   90
should so much resemble his: the same newsmonger, the
same passionate lover of a court, the same – But *basta*,
since I must marry her I'll say nothing, because he shall not
laugh at my misfortune.
RHODOPHIL
Well, Palamede, how go the affairs of love? You've seen   95
your mistress?
PALAMEDE
I have so.

---

78 *obligeant, charmant, ravissant* ed. (obligeant, charmant, ravissant Q1)

81 sp *solus* alone
83 *French gibberish* Melantha's speech is an ungodly mixture of French and English,
   just like the language of lawyers, who functioned until the beginning of the
   eighteenth century in a special language derived from the Middle Ages which was a
   mixture of English, Latin and French.
88 *at cuffs* fighting, wrestling
   rising blow This probably means what we would call an 'uppercut', but it certainly
   also has the sexual connotations of erection and copulation.
92 *basta* Palamede has been in Italy as well as France, and this is Italian for 'enough'.

RHODOPHIL
　　And how, and how? Has the old Cupid, your father,
　　chosen well for you? Is he a good woodman?

PALAMEDE
　　She's much handsomer than I could have imagined. In　100
　　short, I love her, and will marry her.

RHODOPHIL
　　Then you are quite off from your other mistress?

PALAMEDE
　　You are mistaken. I intend to love them both, as a reasonable
　　man ought to do. For since all women have their faults and
　　imperfections, 'tis fit that one of them should help out the　105
　　other.

RHODOPHIL
　　This were a blessed doctrine, indeed, if our wives would
　　hear it. But they're their own enemies. If they would suffer
　　us but now and then to make excursions, the benefit of our
　　variety would be theirs. Instead of one continued, lazy,　110
　　tired love, they would, in their turns, have twenty vigorous,
　　fresh, and active loves.

PALAMEDE
　　And I would ask any of them, whether a poor narrow brook,
　　half dry the best part of the year, and running ever one way,
　　be to be compared to a lusty stream, that has ebbs and flows?　115

RHODOPHIL
　　Ay, or is half so profitable for navigation?

Enter DORALICE, *walking by and reading*

PALAMEDE
　　'Ods my life, Rhodophil, will you keep my counsel?

RHODOPHIL
　　Yes: where's the secret?

---

99 *woodman* huntsman; sometimes used figuratively, as here, of a hunter of women
109–10 *benefit...theirs* Just as the men had mistresses, so the women would have freshly
　　lustful lovers.
113–15 *And...flows* Palamede's words clearly have a sexual connotation. Repeated
　　copulation with a husband becomes a listless thing, whereas the abrupt and stolen
　　lust of a lover is full of desire and then sudden absence. There is probably even a
　　precise reference to ejaculation.
116 *navigation* The boat rides on the water as the man on the woman.
117 *'Ods my life* God's my life

PALAMEDE (*showing* DORALICE)
>   There 'tis. I may tell you, as my friend, *sub sigillo* &c., this
>   is that very numerical lady with whom I am in love.   120
RHODOPHIL (*aside*)
>   By all that's virtuous, my wife!
PALAMEDE
>   You look strangely. How do you like her? Is she not very
>   handsome?
RHODOPHIL (*aside*)
>   Sure he abuses me. (*to him*) Why the devil do you ask my
>   judgment?   125
PALAMEDE
>   You are so dogged now, you think no man's mistress
>   handsome but your own. Come, you shall hear her talk too;
>   she has wit, I assure you.
RHODOPHIL (*going back*)
>   This is too much, Palamede.
PALAMADE (*pulling him forward*)
>   Prithee do not hang back so: of an old tried lover, thou art   130
>   the most bashful fellow!
DORALICE (*looking up*)
>   Were you so near and would not speak, dear husband?
PALAMEDE (*aside*)
>   Husband, quoth a! I have cut out a fine piece of work for
>   myself.
RHODOPHIL
>   Pray, spouse, how long have you been acquainted with this   135
>   gentleman?
DORALICE
>   Who, I acquainted with this stranger? To my best
>   knowledge, I never saw him before.

Enter MELANTHA *at the other end*

PALAMEDE (*aside*)
>   Thanks, Fortune, thou hast helped me.

---

119 *sub sigillo* under the seal. This could mean simply 'on oath not to reveal it', but is
more probably a precise Catholic reference to the seal of the confessional, which
binds a priest under pain of mortal sin not to reveal what the penitent confesses to
him. Catholicism was fashionable and illicit at the court of Charles II, like sex;
Dryden himself became a Catholic in 1686.
120 *numerical* identical
126 *dogged* obstinate, unyielding
130 *of an old* We would say 'for an old'.

RHODOPHIL

    Palamede, this must not pass so. I must know your mistress   140
a little better.

PALAMEDE

    It shall be your own fault else. Come, I'll introduce you.

RHODOPHIL

    Introduce me! Where?

PALAMEDE (*pointing to* MELANTHA, *who swiftly passes over the
stage*) There. To my mistress.

RHODOPHIL

    Who? Melantha! O heavens, I did not see her.   145

PALAMEDE

    But I did: I am an eagle where I love. I have seen her this
half hour.

DORALICE (*aside*)

    I find he has wit, he has got off so readily; but it would
anger me, if he should love Melantha.

RHODOPHIL (*aside*)

    Now I could even wish it were my wife he loved. I find he's   150
to be married to my mistress.

PALAMEDE

    Shall I run after, and fetch her back again, to present you to
her?

RHODOPHIL

    No, you need not. I have the honour to have some small
acquaintance with her.   155

PALAMEDE (*aside*)

    O Jupiter! What a blockhead was I not to find it out! My
wife that must be, is his mistress. I did a little suspect it
before. Well, I must marry her, because she's handsome,
and because I hate to be disinherited for a younger brother,
which I am sure I shall be if I disobey. And yet I must keep   160
in with Rhodophil, because I love his wife. (*to* RHODOPHIL)
I must desire you to make my excuse to your lady, if I have
been so unfortunate to cause any mistake; and, withal, to
beg the honour of being known to her.

RHODOPHIL

    O, that's but reason. Hark you, spouse, pray look upon   165
this gentleman as my friend; whom, to my knowledge, you
have never seen before this hour.

159 *for* in favour of

DORALICE
  I'm so obedient a wife, Sir, that my husband's commands
  shall ever be a law to me.

Enter MELANTHA *again, hastily, and runs to embrace* DORALICE

MELANTHA
  O, my dear, I was just going to pay my *devoirs* to you. I had   170
  not time this morning, for making my court to the king,
  and our new prince. Well, never nation was so happy, and
  all that, in a young prince. And he's the kindest person in
  the world to me, let me die if he is not.
DORALICE
  He has been bred up far from court, and therefore –   175
MELANTHA
  That imports not. Though he has not seen the *grand monde*,
  and all that, let me die but he has the air of the court, most
  absolutely.
PALAMEDE
  But yet, Madam, he –
MELANTHA
  O, servant, you can testify that I am in his good graces.   180
  Well, I cannot stay long with you, because I have promised
  him this afternoon to – (*whispers to* DORALICE) But hark
  you, my dear, I'll tell you a secret.
RHODOPHIL (*aside*)
  The devil's in me, that I must love this woman.
PALAMEDE (*aside*)
  The devil's in me, that I must marry this woman.   185
MELANTHA (*raising her voice*)
  So the prince and I – [*to* DORALICE *again*] But you must make
  a secret of this, my dear, for I would not for the world your
  husband should hear it, or my tyrant there that must be.
PALAMEDE (*aside*)
  Well, fair impertinent, your whisper is not lost. We hear you.
DORALICE
  I understand then, that –   190

---

170 *devoirs* (devoirs Q1)

---

170 *devoirs* respects
171 *for* because of
172–3 *and all that* This man about town phrase is one of Bayes' characteristic expressions
  in *The Rehearsal*. It is common, too, in the speech of Failer in Dryden's *The Wild
  Gallant* (1663).

MELANTHA
> I'll tell you, my dear, the prince took me by the hand, and
> pressed it *à la dérobée*, because the king was near, made the
> *doux yeux* to me and, *en suite*, said a thousand *galanteries*, or
> let me die, my dear.

DORALICE
> Then I am sure you –   195

MELANTHA
> You are mistaken, my dear.

DORALICE
> What, before I speak?

MELANTHA
> But I know your meaning. You think, my dear, that I
> assumed something of *fierté* into my countenance, to *rebute*
> him; but, quite contrary, I regarded him, I know not how   200
> to express it in our dull Sicilian language, *d'un air enjoué;*
> and said nothing but *à d'autre, à d'autre*, and that it was all
> *grimace*, and would not pass upon me.

> *Enter* ARTEMIS; MELANTHA *sees her,*
> *and runs away from* DORALICE

> (*to* ARTEMIS) My dear, I must beg your pardon. I was just
> making a loose from Doralice, to pay my respects to you.   205
> Let me die if I ever pass time so agreeably as in your com-
> pany, and if I would leave it for any lady's in Sicily.

ARTEMIS
> The Princess Amalthea is coming this way.

192 *à la* D (*al a* Q1)
193 *en* ed. (*in* Q1)
     galanteries ed. (Gallanteries Q1)
197 *What,* Q1a (What Q1)
201 *enjoué* ed. (*enjouué* Q1)
202 *à d'autre, à d'autre* ed. (*ad autre, ad autre* Q1)

---

192 *à la dérobée* secretly
193 *doux yeux* amorous eyes
     en suite to follow that
199 *fierté* pride
     rebute repulse
201 *d'un air enjoué* with a sportive air
202 *à d'autre, à d'autre* go and tell that to someone else who might believe it. The
     nearest English equivalent, though the tone is quite wrong, would be 'tell that to
     the marines'. The phrase is spelt with a final s at V. i. 145.
203 *grimace* done as playful deception
     pass upon convince
205 *making a loose* getting away

Enter AMALTHEA; MELANTHA *runs to her*

MELANTHA

O dear Madam! I have been at your lodgings, in my new
calèche, so often, to tell you of a new *amour*, betwixt two   210
persons whom you would little suspect for it, that, let me
die if one of my coach-horses be not dead, and another
quite tired and sunk under the *fatigue*.

AMALTHEA

O, Melantha, I can tell you news. The prince is coming this
way.   215

MELANTHA

The prince, O sweet prince! He and I are to – and I forgot
it. – Your pardon, sweet Madam, for my abruptness. Adieu,
my dears. Servant, Rhodophil; servant, servant, servant all.
                                                                         Exit running

AMALTHEA (*whispers*)

Rhodophil, a word with you.

DORALICE (*to* PALAMEDE)

Why do you not follow your mistress, Sir?   220

PALAMEDE

Follow her? Why, at this rate she'll be at the Indies within
this half hour.

DORALICE

However, if you can't follow her all day, you'll meet her at
night, I hope?

PALAMEDE

But can you, in charity, suffer me to be so mortified, without   225
affording me some relief? If it be but to punish that sign of
a husband there, that lazy matrimony, that dull insipid
taste, who leaves such delicious fare at home to dine abroad,
on worse meat, and to pay dear for it into the bargain.

DORALICE

All this is in vain. Assure yourself, I will never admit of   230
any visit from you in private.

218 *Rhodophil* Q2 (*Rodophil* Q1)
219 *Rhodophil* Q2 (*Rodophil* Q1)

---

210 *calèche* a fashionable kind of light carriage introduced from France
218 *servant...all* Melantha's leavetaking ('servant' short for 'your servant') is both
       voluble and comically abbreviated. In reality, of course, she is constantly herself a
       servant, running after great ones.
226–7 *sign of a husband* merely outward show of a husband
227 *matrimony* Rhodophil is metamorphosed jokily into the allegorical figure of
       Matrimony, signifying the dullness of dutiful sex.

PALAMEDE
That is to tell me, in other words, my condition is desperate.
DORALICE
I think you in so ill a condition, that I am resolved to pray for
you, this very evening, in the close walk, behind the
terrace; for that's a private place, and there I am sure nobody   235
will disturb my devotions. And so, good night, Sir.

Exit

PALAMEDE
This is the newest way of making an appointment I ever
heard of. Let women alone to contrive the means; I find we
are but dunces to them. Well, I will not be so profane a
wretch as to interrupt her devotions; but to make them   240
more effectual, I'll down upon my knees, and endeavour
to join my own with them.

Exit

AMALTHEA (*to* RHODOPHIL)
I know already they do not love each other; and that my
brother acts but a forced obedience to the king's commands; so that, if a quarrel should arise betwixt the prince   245
and him, I were most miserable on both sides.
RHODOPHIL
There shall be nothing wanting in me, Madam, to prevent
so sad a consequence.

Enter [POLYDAMAS] *the king,* LEONIDAS;
the king whispers [*to*] AMALTHEA

(*to himself*) I begin to hate this Palamede, because he is to
marry my mistress: yet break with him I dare not, for fear   250
of being quite excluded from her company. 'Tis a hard case
when a man must go by his rival to his mistress, but 'tis at
worst but using him like a pair of heavy boots in a dirty
journey; after I have fouled him all day, I'll throw him off
at night.   255

Exit

AMALTHEA (*to the king*)
This honour is too great for me to hope.
POLYDAMAS
You shall this hour have the assurance of it.
Leonidas, come hither; you have heard,
I doubt not, that the father of this princess
Was my most faithful friend, while I was yet   260

---

241 *down upon my knees* This would not only be the preparation for prayer but for
copulation, the joining of bodies not souls.

A private man; and when I did assume
This crown, he served me in that high attempt.
You see, then, to what gratitude obliges me;
Make your addresses to her.

LEONIDAS
Sir, I am yet too young to be a courtier;   265
I should too much betray my ignorance,
And want of breeding, to so fair a lady.

AMALTHEA
Your language speaks you not bred up in deserts,
But in the softness of some Asian court,
Where luxury and ease invent kind words,   270
To cozen tender virgins of their hearts.

POLYDAMAS
You need not doubt
But in what words so'er a prince can offer
His crown and person, they will be received.
You know my pleasure, and you know your duty.   275

LEONIDAS
Yes, Sir, I shall obey, in what I can.

POLYDAMAS
In what you can, Leonidas? Consider,
He's both your king, and father, who commands you.
Besides, what is there hard in my injunction?

LEONIDAS
'Tis hard to have my inclination forced.   280
I would not marry, Sir; and, when I do,
I hope you'll give me freedom in my choice.

POLYDAMAS
View well this lady,
Whose mind as much transcends her beauteous face,
As that excels all others.   285

AMALTHEA
My beauty, as it ne'er could merit love,
So neither can it beg: and Sir, you may
Believe that what the king has offered you,
I should refuse, did I not value more
Your person than your crown.

LEONIDAS   Think it not pride,   290
Or my new fortunes swell me to contemn you;
Think less, that I want eyes to see your beauty;
And least of all think duty wanting in me
To obey a father's will: but –

POLYDAMAS   But what, Leonidas?
For I must know your reason; and be sure   295

It be convincing too.
LEONIDAS   Sir, ask the stars,
    Which have imposed love on us, like a fate,
    Why minds are bent to one, and fly another?
    Ask why all beauties cannot move all hearts.
    For though there may   300
    Be made a rule for colour, or for feature;
    There can be none for liking.
POLYDAMAS
    Leonidas, you owe me more
    Than to oppose your liking to my pleasure.
LEONIDAS
    I owe you all things, Sir; but something too   305
    I owe myself.
POLYDAMAS
    You shall dispute no more; I am a king,
    And I will be obeyed.
LEONIDAS
    You are a king, Sir, but you are no god;
    Or if you were, you could not force my will.   310
POLYDAMAS (*aside*)
    But you are just, you gods; O you are just,
    In punishing the crimes of my rebellion
    With a rebellious son!
    Yet I can punish him, as you do me.
    [*to* LEONIDAS] Leonidas, there is no jesting with   315
    My will. I ne'er had done so much to gain
    A crown, but to be absolute in all things.
AMALTHEA
    O Sir, be not so much a king, as to
    Forget you are a father. Soft indulgence
    Becomes that name. Though nature gives you power   320
    To bind his duty, 'tis with silken bonds.
    Command him, then, as you command yourself:
    He is as much a part of you, as are
    Your appetite, and will, and those you force not,
    But gently bend, and make them pliant to your reason.   325
POLYDAMAS
    It may be I have used too rough a way.
    Forgive me, my Leonidas; I know
    I lie as open to the gusts of passion,
    As the bare shore to every beating surge.

---

321 *his duty* Leonidas' duty is that of a son, as distinct from that of a subject which is
    bound with kingly power not fatherly affection.

I will not force thee now; but I intreat thee,   330
Absolve a father's vow to this fair virgin:
A vow which hopes of having such a son
First caused.
LEONIDAS
Show not my disobedience by your prayers,
For I must still deny you, though I now   335
Appear more guilty to myself than you.
I have some reasons, which I cannot utter,
That force my disobedience; yet I mourn
To death, that the first thing you e'er enjoined me,
Should be that only one command in nature   340
Which I could not obey.
POLYDAMAS
I did descend too much below myself
When I intreated him. Hence, to thy desert,
Thou art not my son, or art not fit to be.
AMALTHEA (*kneeling*)
Great Sir, I humbly beg you, make not me   345
The cause of your displeasure. I absolve
Your vow. Far, far from me be such designs,
So wretched a desire of being great,
By making him unhappy. You may see
Something so noble in the prince his nature,   350
As grieves him more not to obey, than you
That you are not obeyed.
POLYDAMAS   Then, for your sake,
I'll give him one day longer, to consider
Not to deny; for my resolves are firm
As Fate, that cannot change.
                    Exeunt king and AMALTHEA
LEONIDAS   And so are mine.   355
This beauteous princess, charming as she is,
Could never make me happy. I must first
Be false to my Palmyra, and then wretched.
But, then, a father's anger!
Suppose he should recede from his own vow,   360
He never would permit me to keep mine.

Enter PALMYRA; ARGALEON *following her, a little after*

---

331 *Absolve* perform, make good
346 *absolve* dispense you from
350 *prince his* prince's; a slightly solemn and old-fashioned version of the ordinary
    possessive

See, she appears!
I'll think no more of anything, but her.
Yet I have one hour good ere I am wretched.
But, Oh! Argaleon follows her! so night   365
Treads on the footsteps of a winter's sun,
And stalks all black behind him.

PALMYRA   O Leonidas,
(For I must call you still by that dear name)
Free me from this bad man.

LEONIDAS
I hope he dares not be injurious to you.   370

ARGALEON
I rather was injurious to myself,
Than her.

LEONIDAS
That must be judged when I hear what you said.

ARGALEON
I think you need not give yourself that trouble:
It concerned us alone.   375

LEONIDAS
You answer saucily, and indirectly.
What interest can you pretend in her?

ARGALEON
It may be, Sir, I made her some expressions
Which I would not repeat, because they were
Below my rank, to one of hers.   380

LEONIDAS
What did he say, Palmyra?

PALMYRA
I'll tell you all. First, he began to look,
And then he sighed, and then he looked again;
At last, he said my eyes wounded his heart:
And, after that, he talked of flames, and fires,   385
And such strange words, that I believed he conjured.

LEONIDAS
O my heart! Leave me, Argaleon.

ARGALEON
Come, sweet Palmyra,
I will instruct you better in my meaning.
You see he would be private.

LEONIDAS   Go yourself,   390
And leave her here.

---

364 *hour* short time. He has actually just been given a day.

ARGALEON   Alas, she's ignorant,
  And is not fit to entertain a prince.
LEONIDAS
  First learn what's fit for you; that's to obey.
ARGALEON
  I know my duty is to wait on you.
  A great king's son, like you, ought to forget   395
  Such mean converse.
LEONIDAS   What? A disputing subject?
  Hence; or my sword shall do me justice on thee.
ARGALEON (*going*)
  Yet I may find a time –
LEONIDAS (*going after him*)   What's that you mutter,
  To find a time?
ARGALEON   To wait on you again –
  (*softly*) In the mean while I'll watch you.   400
                       Exit, and watches during the scene
LEONIDAS
  How precious are the hours of love in courts!
  In cottages, where love has all the day,
  Full, and at ease, he throws it half away.
  Time gives himself, and is not valued, there;
  But sells, at mighty rates, each minute here.   405
  There, he is lazy, unemployed, and slow;
  Here, he's more swift, and yet has more to do.
  So many of his hours in public move,
  That few are left for privacy, and love.
PALMYRA
  The sun, methinks, shines faint and dimly here;   410
  Light is not half so long, nor half so clear.
  But, Oh! When every day was yours and mine,
  How early up! What haste he made to shine!
LEONIDAS
  Such golden days no prince must hope to see,
  Whose every subject is more blessed than he.   415
PALMYRA
  Do you remember, when their tasks were done,
  How all the youth did to our cottage run?
  While winter winds were whistling loud without,
  Our cheerful hearth was circled round about.

401 *How precious...* From here to the end of Act II, the echo is of Florizel and Perdita in
    The Winter's Tale IV. iv. See note at III. i. 297.

With strokes in ashes maids their lovers drew,   420
And still you fell to me, and I to you.

LEONIDAS

When love did of my heart possession take,
I was so young, my soul was scarce awake.
I cannot tell when first I thought you fair,
But sucked in love insensibly as air.   425

PALMYRA

I know too well when first my love began,
When, at our wake, you for the chaplet ran.
Then I was made the lady of the May,
And with the garland at the goal did stay.
Still as you ran, I kept you full in view;   430
I hoped, and wished, and ran, methought, for you.
As you came near, I hastily did rise,
And stretched my arm outright, that held the prize.
The custom was to kiss whom I should crown:
You kneeled; and in my lap your head laid down.   435
I blushed, and blushed, and did the kiss delay:
At last, my subjects forced me to obey;
But when I gave the crown, and then the kiss,
I scarce had breath to say, take that – and this.

LEONIDAS

I felt the while a pleasing kind of smart;   440
The kiss went, tingling, to my very heart.
When it was gone, the sense of it did stay;
The sweetness clinged upon my lips all day,
Like drops of honey, loath to fall away.

PALMYRA

Life, like a prodigal, gave all his store   445
To my first youth, and now can give no more.
You are a prince; and, in that high degree,
No longer must converse with humble me.

LEONIDAS

'Twas to my loss the gods that title gave;
A tyrant's son is doubly born a slave.   450
He gives a crown; but to prevent my life
From being happy, loads it with a wife.

---

420 *strokes in ashes* The girls made marks in the ashes which could be interpreted as the names of their lovers.

427 *wake* The local annual festival of an English parish, observed on the feast of the patron saint of the church. Such festivals were forbidden during the Cromwellian interregnum.

chaplet garland of victory

PALMYRA
  Speak quickly. What have you resolved to do?
LEONIDAS
  To keep my faith inviolate to you.
  He threatens me with exile, and with shame,   455
  To lose my birthright, and a prince his name;
  But there's a blessing which he did not mean,
  To send me back to love and you again.
PALMYRA
  Why was not I a princess for your sake?
  But heaven no more such miracles can make: 460
  And, since that cannot, this must never be;
  You shall not lose a crown for love of me.
  Live happy, and a nobler choice pursue;
  I shall complain of fate, but not of you.
LEONIDAS
  Can you so easily without me live?   465
  Or could you take the counsel which you give?
  Were you a princess would you not be true?
PALMYRA
  I would; but cannot merit it from you.
LEONIDAS
  Did you not merit, as you do, my heart,
  Love gives esteem, and then it gives desert.   470
  But if I basely could forget my vow,
  Poor helpless Innocence, what would you do?
PALMYRA
  In woods, and plains, where first my love began,
  There would I live, retired from faithless man.
  I'd sit all day within some lonely shade,   475
  Or that close arbour which your hands have made.
  I'd search the groves, and every tree, to find
  Where you had carved our names upon the rind.
  Your hook, your scrip, all that was yours, I'd keep,
  And lay them by me when I went to sleep.   480
  Thus would I live: and maidens when I die
  Upon my hearse white true-love-knots should tie:
  And thus my tomb should be inscribed above,
  Here the forsaken virgin rests from love.
LEONIDAS
  Think not that time or fate shall e'er divide   485
  Those hearts, which love and mutual vows have tied.

479 *hook* crook
    scrip shepherd's wallet

But we must part; farewell, my love.
PALMYRA   Till when?
LEONIDAS
Till the next age of hours we meet again.
Meantime – we may –
When near each other we in public stand,   490
Contrive to catch a look or steal a hand.
Fancy will every touch, and glance improve;
And draw the most spirituous parts of love.
Our souls sit close and silently within,
And their own web from their own entrails spin.   495
And when eyes meet far off, our sense is such,
That, spider-like, we feel the tenderest touch.

                                        Exeunt

Act III, Scene i

Enter RHODOPHIL, *meeting* DORALICE *and* ARTEMIS
RHODOPHIL *and* DORALICE *embrace*

RHODOPHIL
My own dear heart!
DORALICE
My own true love! (*she starts back*) I had forgot myself to be
so kind. Indeed I am very angry with you, dear; you are
come home an hour after you appointed. If you had stayed
a minute longer, (*embracing him*) I was just considering   5
whether I should stab, hang, or drown myself.
RHODOPHIL
Nothing but the king's business could have hindered me; and
I was so vexed, that I was just laying down my commission,
(*kissing her hand*) rather than have failed my dear.
ARTEMIS
Why, this is love as it should be, betwixt man and wife.   10
Such another couple would bring marriage into fashion
again. But is it always thus betwixt you?
RHODOPHIL
Always thus! This is nothing. I tell you there is not such a
pair of turtles in all Sicily. There is such an eternal cooing

---

488 *Till...again* This slightly obscure and high-flown formulation seems to mean 'till
   the hours have gone by which separate us from our next meeting, which will seem
   like an age.'
  14 *turtles* turtledoves. They were proverbial for their fidelity to their mates.

and kissing betwixt us, that indeed it is scandalous before   15
civil company.

DORALICE

Well, if I had imagined I should have been this fond fool, I
would never have married the man I loved. I married to be
happy, and have made myself miserable by over-loving.
Nay and now my case is desperate, for I have been married   20
above these two years, and find myself every day worse and
worse in love. Nothing but madness can be the end on't.

ARTEMIS

Dote on, to the extremity, and you are happy.

DORALICE

He deserves so infinitely much that, the truth is, there can
be no doting in the matter. But to love well, I confess,   25
is a work that pays itself. 'Tis telling gold, and after taking
it for one's pains.

RHODOPHIL

By that I should be a very covetous person, for I am ever
pulling out my money, and putting it into my pocket again.

DORALICE

O dear Rhodophil!   30

RHODOPHIL

O sweet Doralice! (*embracing each other*)

ARTEMIS (*aside*)

Nay, I am resolved I'll never interrupt lovers. I'll leave
them as happy as I found them.

                                              Steals away

RHODOPHIL (*looking up*)

What, is she gone?

DORALICE

Yes; and without taking leave.   35

RHODOPHIL (*parting from her*)

Then there's enough for this time.

DORALICE

Yes sure, the scene's done, I take it.

*They walk contrary ways on the stage, he with his hands in his
pocket whistling, she singing a dull melancholy tune*

RHODOPHIL

Pox o' your dull tune; a man can't think for you.

36 *time.* Q2 (time Q1)

26–7 *telling...pains* counting over gold and then taking the gold as payment for that
labour

DORALICE
Pox 'o your damned whistling; you can neither be company
to me yourself, nor leave me to the freedom of my own fancy.   40
RHODOPHIL
Well, thou art the most provoking wife!
DORALICE
Well, thou art the dullest husband; thou art never to be
provoked.
RHODOPHIL
I was never thought dull till I married thee; and now thou
hast made an old knife of me; thou hast whetted me so long   45
till I have no edge left.
DORALICE
I see you are in the husband's fashion. You reserve all your
good humours for your mistresses, and keep your ill for
your wives.
RHODOPHIL
Prithee leave me to my own cogitations. I am thinking over   50
all my sins, to find for which of them it was I married thee.
DORALICE
Whatever your sin was, mine's the punishment.
RHODOPHIL
My comfort is, thou art not immortal; and when that blessed,
that divine day comes, of thy departure, I'm resolved I'll
make one holy-day more in the almanac, for thy sake.   55
DORALICE
Ay, you had need make a holy-day for me, for I am sure
you have made me a martyr.
RHODOPHIL
Then, setting my victorious foot upon thy head, in the first
hour of thy silence, (that is, the first hour thou art dead, for
I despair of it before) I will swear by thy ghost, an oath as   60
terrible to me as Styx is to the gods, never more to be in
danger of the banes of matrimony.

---

43 *provoked*. Q2 (provok'd, Q1)

---

43 *provoked* There is a sexual innuendo here, in the sense of 'aroused'. The innuendo
continues into the next speech.
61 *Styx is to the gods* When a god swore falsely by Styx, the river of the underworld,
he was made to drink a draught of its water, which made him lie speechless for a
year.
62 *banes* I have left unmodernised this perfectly usual seventeenth-century spelling
for 'banns' on the grounds that the word is clearly meant to pun with 'bane' = woe.

DORALICE

And I am resolved to marry the very same day thou diest, if
it be but to show how little I'm concerned for thee.

RHODOPHIL

Prithee, Doralice, why do we quarrel thus a-days? Ha? This　65
is but a kind of heathenish life, and does not answer the ends
of marriage. If I have erred, propound what reasonable
atonement may be made, before we sleep, and I shall not be
refractory: but withal consider I have been married these
three years, and be not too tyrannical.　70

DORALICE

What should you talk of a peace abed, when you can give
no security for performance of articles?

RHODOPHIL

Then, since we must live together, and both of us stand
upon our terms, as to matter of dying first, let us make
ourselves as merry as we can with our misfortunes. Why　75
there's the devil on't! If thou could'st make my enjoying
thee but a little less easy, or a little more unlawful, thou
shouldst see what a termagant lover I would prove. I have
taken such pains to enjoy thee, Doralice, that I have
fancied thee all the fine women in the town, to help me out.　80
But now there's none left for me to think on, my imagination is quite jaded. Thou art a wife, and thou wilt be a wife,
and I can make thee another no longer.

Exit RHODOPHIL

DORALICE

Well, since thou art a husband, and wilt be a husband, I'll
try if I can find out another! 'Tis a pretty time we women　85
have on't, to be made widows while we are married. Our
husbands think it reasonable to complain that we are the
same, and the same to them, when we have more reason to
complain, that they are not the same to us. Because they
cannot feed on one dish, therefore we must be starved. 'Tis　90

---

65 *a-days* day after day

72 *for performance of articles* that you will keep to the terms of the agreement. But the
sexual innuendo in 'performance' is also clear, and indeed the chief meaning.

73–4 *stand…first* are resolved what we shall do when the other dies first

78 *termagant lover* Termagant was the name of an imaginary deity thought in
mediaeval Christendom to be worshipped by Mohammedans. He was represented
as savage and overbearing. Rhodophil is saying what a violently lustful lover he
would be.

79–80 *pains…out* In copulating with Doralice, Rhodophil has tried to give an edge to
his lust by pretending she was a pretty woman illicitly conquered.

enough that they have a sufficient ordinary provided, and
a table ready spread for them. If they cannot fall to and eat
heartily, the fault is theirs; and 'tis pity, methinks, that the
good creature should be lost, when many a poor sinner
would be glad on't.   95

Enter MELANTHA, *and* ARTEMIS *to her*

MELANTHA
Dear, my dear, pity me. I am so *chagrin* today, and have
had the most signal *affront* at court! I went this afternoon
to do my *devoir* to Princess Amalthea, found her, conversed
with her, and helped to make her court some half an hour;
after which she went to take the air, chose out two ladies to   100
go with her that came in after me, and left me most
barbarously behind her.

ARTEMIS
You are the less to be pitied, Melantha, because you subject
yourself to these affronts by coming perpetually to court,
where you have no business nor employment.   105

MELANTHA
I declare, I had rather of the two, be *raillied*, nay *mal traitée*
at court than be deified in the town: for assuredly nothing
can be so *ridicule* as a mere town-lady.

92   *to* Q4 (too Q1)
96   *chagrin* ed. (chagrin Q1)
97   *affront* (affront Q1)
98   *devoir* (devoir Q1)

91   *ordinary* a public meal regularly provided at a fixed price in an eating-house or
     tavern
94   *creature* food
96   *chagrin* disquieted, troubled
99   *helped...court* was one of those paying court to her. Melantha prefers the expression
     'make court' because it is closer to the French 'faire la cour'.
104 *affronts* The word can be English or French, and no doubt there was meant to be a
     distinct difference between the pronunciation Artemis gives it and the way
     Melantha has just said it. This would have been a nice little dramatic moment, with
     perhaps a final shot at III. i. 170.
106 *raillied* scoffed at. The spelling (for English 'rallied') indicates another word, like
     'affront', stranded halfway between English and French in Melantha's speech.
     mal traitée badly treated
108 *ridicule* ridiculous
     town-lady See note at I. i. 182.

DORALICE

Especially at court. How I have seen them crowd and sweat
in the drawing-room on a holiday-night! For that's their   110
time to swarm, and invade the presence. O, how they catch
at a bow, or any little salute from a courtier, to make show
of their acquaintance! And rather than be thought to be
quite unknown, they curtsey to one another. But they take
true pains to come near the circle, and press and peep upon   115
the princess, to write letters into the country how she was
dressed, while the ladies that stand about make their court
to her with abusing them.

ARTEMIS

These are sad truths, Melantha; and therefore I would
even advise you to quit the court, and live either wholly in   120
the town, or if you like not that, in the country.

DORALICE

In the country! Nay, that's to fall beneath the town, for
they live there upon our offals here. Their entertainment
of wit is only the remembrance of what they had when they
were last in town. They live this year upon the last year's   125
knowledge as their cattle do all night by chewing the cud of
what they eat in the afternoon.

MELANTHA

And they tell, for news, such unlikely stories. A letter from
one of us is such a present to them, that the poor souls wait
for the carrier's day with such devotion that they cannot   130
sleep the night before.

ARTEMIS

No more than I can, the night before I am to go a journey.

---

110 *holiday-night* The Church of England celebrated during the year about thirty feast
   days in addition to the usual Sundays; and on these holy days the court was open in
   the evening to visitors of a certain class from outside. Doralice's speech here, with
   the town-ladies swarming like bees when allowed into the court, was no doubt
   particularly for the amusement of the court element in the audience of a theatre
   consciously the *King's* Company in the Theatre *Royal* putting on a play by the poet
   laureate. See note at Prologue 24.

115 *the circle* the name for the assembly of people immediately sitting or standing round
   the royal presence

130 *carrier's day* The common carriers normally transported goods and parcels, and
   were not allowed to carry letters as a regular part of their service. Letters and
   packets were delivered by the relatively speedy postal system established from the
   beginning of the sixteenth century. Perhaps the indication here is that these 'poor
   souls' lived in such remote parts that the ordinary post would not reach them, only
   the much slower carrier.

DORALICE

Or I, before I am to try on a new gown.

MELANTHA

A song that's stale here will be new there a twelvemonth
hence; and if a man of the town by chance come amongst   135
them, he's reverenced for teaching them the tune.

DORALICE

A friend of mine, who makes songs sometimes, came lately
out of the west, and vowed he was so put out of countenance
with a song of his. For at the first country gentleman's he
visited, he saw three tailors crosslegged upon the table in the   140
hall, who were tearing out as loud as ever they could sing:
– *After the pangs of a desperate lover*, &c.
And all that day he heard nothing else but the daughters of
the house and the maids humming it over in every corner,
and the father whistling it.   145

ARTEMIS

Indeed I have observed of myself, that when I am out of
town but a fortnight, I am so humble that I would receive a
letter from my tailor or mercer for a favour.

MELANTHA

When I have been at grass in the summer, and am new
come up again, methinks I'm to be turned into *ridicule* by   150
all that see me; but when I have been once or twice at court,
I begin to value myself again, and to despise my country
acquaintance.

ARTEMIS

There are places where all people may be adored, and we
ought to know ourselves so well as to choose them.   155

DORALICE

That's very true. Your little courtier's wife, who speaks to
the king but once a month, need but go to a town-lady, and
there she may vapour, and cry, *The king and I*, at every

---

142 *&c.* Q3 (*&c.* Q1)

---

140 *three tailors* Why tailors? Perhaps because a tailor, owing to his womanly trade, was
not thought much of a man, or as a consequence much of a lover. The proverbial
saying was that it takes many tailors to make one proper man (M.P.Tilley, *A
Dictionary of the Proverbs in England in the Sixteenth and Seventeenth Centuries*, Ann
Arbor, 1950, T.23). A tailor called Tom Thimble in *The Rehearsal* is thought unlikely to make a good lover (III.i.26–9). The song the tailors sing is by Dryden,
from *An Evening's Love* (1668) II.i.
158 *vapour* talk in a grandiloquent way

word. Your town-lady, who is laughed at in the circle,
takes her coach into the city, and there she's called your   160
Honour, and has a banquet from the merchant's wife,
whom she laughs at for her kindness. And as for my finical
cit, she removes but to her country house, and there insults
over the country gentlewoman that never comes up; who
treats her with frumity and custard, and opens her dear   165
bottle of *mirabilis* beside, for a jill-glass of it at parting.

ARTEMIS
At last, I see, we shall leave Melantha where we found her;
for by your description of the town and country, they are
become more dreadful to her than the court, where she was
affronted. But you forget we are to wait on the Princess   170
Amalthea. Come, Doralice.

DORALICE
Farewell, Melantha.

MELANTHA
Adieu, my dear.

ARTEMIS
You are out of charity with her, and therefore I shall not
give your service.   175

MELANTHA
Do not omit it, I beseech you, for I have such a *tender* for
the court, that I love it even from the drawing-room to the
lobby, and can never be *rebutée* by any usage. But hark
you, my dears, one thing I had forgot of great concernment.

DORALICE
Quickly then, we are in haste.   180

---

176 *tender* (tender Q1)

162–3 *finical cit* affectedly fastidious citizen, or city dweller. The abbreviation 'cit' was
    derogatory.
165 *frumity* a country dish made of wheat boiled in milk and seasoned
166 *mirabilis* This is short for *aqua mirabilis*, a cordial composed, according to
    Johnson's *Dictionary*, of 'cloves, galangals, cubebs, mace, cardomums, nutmegs,
    ginger, and spirit of wine, digested twenty four hours, then distilled.'
    jill-glass a small measure, containing a quarter of a pint
176 *tender* This absolute use of the adjective, to mean 'tender feeling', is known in the
    seventeenth century. Doubtless Melantha pronounces it with the French noun
    'tendre' in mind.
178 *rebutée* repulsed

MELANTHA

Do not call it my service, that's too vulgar; but do my *baise mains* to the Princess Amalthea; that is *spirituelle!*

DORALICE

To do you service then, we will *prendre* the *carrosse* to court, and do your *baise mains* to the Princess Amalthea, in your phrase *spirituellé*.   185

Exeunt ARTEMIS *and* DORALICE

Enter PHILOTIS *with a paper in her hand*

MELANTHA

O, are you there, *minion*? And, well, are not you a most precious damsel, to retard all my visits for want of language, when you know you are paid so well for furnishing me with new words for my daily conversation? Let me die if I have not run the *risque* already, to speak like one of the vulgar;   190 and if I have one phrase left in all my store that is not threadbare and *usé*, and fit for nothing but to be thrown to peasants.

PHILOTIS

Indeed, Madam, I have been very diligent in my vocation; but you have so drained all the French plays and romances,   195 that they are not able to supply you with words for your daily expenses.

MELANTHA

Drained? What a word's there! *Epuisé*, you sot you. Come, produce your morning's work.

PHILOTIS *(shows the paper)*

'Tis here, Madam.   200

MELANTHA

O, my Venus! Fourteen or fifteen words to serve me a

---

186 *minion* (Minion Q1)
190 *risque* ed. (risque Q1)
192 *and* (& Q1)
    usé Q4 (*usè* Q1)
198 *Epuisé* (*Epuisée* Q1)

181–2 *baise mains* kiss hands
182 *spirituelle* witty, elegant
183 *prendre the carrosse* take the carriage
185 *spirituellé* This seems a deliberately and satirically anglicised attempt to form the adverb, rather like the half and half speech of '*prendre* the *carrosse*'.
186 *minion* my dear; consciously from the French 'mignon'
190 *to speak* of speaking
192 *usé* worn out

whole day! Let me die, at this rate I cannot last till night.
Come, read your words: twenty to one half of them will not
pass muster neither.

PHILOTIS (*reads*)
 Sottises.   205

MELANTHA
 Sottises: bon. That's an excellent word to begin withal; as for
 example: he, or she said a thousand *sottises* to me. Proceed.

PHILOTIS
 Figure: as, what a *figure* of a man is there! *Naive*, and *naiveté*.

MELANTHA
 Naive! As how?

PHILOTIS
 Speaking of a thing that was naturally said. It was so *naive*. 210
 Or such an innocent piece of simplicity: 'twas such a *naiveté*.

MELANTHA
 Truce with your interpretations. Make haste.

PHILOTIS
 Foible, chagrin, grimace, embarrasse, double entendre,
 équivoque, éclaircissement, suite, bévue, façon, penchant,
 coup d'étourdi, and *ridicule.*   215

MELANTHA
 Hold, hold. How did they begin?

PHILOTIS
 They began at *sottises*, and ended *en ridicule*.

MELANTHA
 Now give me your paper in my hand, and hold you my glass
 while I practise my postures for the day. (MELANTHA *laughs*
 in the glass) How does that laugh become my face? 220

PHILOTIS
 Sovereignly well, Madam.

---

203 *words* ed. (works Q1)
208 *a figure* ed. (a figure Q1)
214 *suite* (*Suittè* Q1)
 façon ed. (*Facòn* Q1)

---

205 *Sottises* foolish things
213 *Foible* Melantha uses this word (see III.i.257) as a noun, meaning 'weakness,
 weak point'. I have left the French unmodernised here on the grounds that 'foible'
 is now accepted English usage.
214 *équivoque* equivocal
 éclaircissement explanation
 bévue blunder, mistake
 façon manner, way
215 *coup d'étourdi* senseless blunder

MELANTHA

Sovereignly! Let me die, that's not amiss. That word shall
not be yours; I'll invent it and bring it up myself. My new
point gorget shall be yours upon't. Not a word of the word,
I charge you.   225

PHILOTIS

I am dumb, Madam.

MELANTHA (*looking in the glass again*)

That glance, how suits it with my face?

PHILOTIS

'Tis so *languissant.*

MELANTHA

Languissant! That word shall be mine too, and my last
Indian-gown thine for it. (*looks again*) That sigh?   230

PHILOTIS

'Twill make many a man sigh, Madam. 'Tis a mere *incendiary.*

MELANTHA

Take my guimp petticoat for that truth. If thou hast more
of these phrases, let me die but I could give away all my
wardrobe, and go naked for them.

PHILOTIS

Go naked? Then you would be a Venus, Madam. O Jupiter!   235
What had I forgot? This paper was given me by Rhodophil's
page.

MELANTHA (*reading the letter*)

– *Beg the favour from you* – *gratify my passion* – *so far* –
assignation – *in the grotto* – *behind the terrace* – *clock this
evening* – Well, for the *billets doux* there's no man in Sicily   240
must dispute with Rhodophil; they are so French, so *galant,*
and so *tendre,* that I cannot resist the temptation of the
assignation. Now go you away, Philotis; it imports me to
practise what I shall say to my servant when I meet him.
                                                Exit PHILOTIS
Rhodophil, you'll wonder at my assurance to meet you here.   245
Let me die I am so out of breath with coming that I can render

224 *point gorget* (Point Gorget Q1)
237 *you* Q2 (you. Q1)

---

224 *point gorget*   a lace covering for neck and breast
228 *languissant* languishing
230 *Indian-gown* Both men and women of a certain class would discard their formal
     outer garments indoors and wear a 'morning gown' or 'Indian gown'.
231 *mere incendiary* absolute inflamer of passion
232 *guimp* trimmed with lace patterned in a coarser thread

you no reason of it. Then he will make this *repartee:* Madam,
I have no reason to accuse you for that which is so great a
favour to me. Then I reply: but why have you drawn me to
this solitary place? Let me die but I am apprehensive of   250
some violence from you. Then says he: solitude, Madam,
is most fit for lovers; but by this fair hand – Nay, now I vow
you're rude. Sir. O fie, fie, fie; I hope you'll be honourable?
– You'd laugh at me if I should, Madam – What do you
mean to throw me down thus? Ah me! ah, ah, ah.   255

Enter POLYDAMAS, LEONIDAS, *and guards*

O Venus! The king and court. Let me die but I fear they
have found my *foible* and will turn me into *ridicule.*

Exit running

LEONIDAS
Sir, I beseech you.
POLYDAMAS   Do not urge my patience.
LEONIDAS
I'll not deny
But what your spies informed you of, is true: 260
I love the fair Palmyra; but I loved her
Before I knew your title to my blood.

Enter PALMYRA, *guarded*

See, here she comes; and looks, amidst her guards,
Like a weak dove under the falcon's gripe.
O heaven, I cannot bear it.
POLYDAMAS   Maid, come hither.   265
Have you presumed so far, as to receive
My son's affection?
PALMYRA
Alas, what shall I answer? To confess it
Will raise a blush upon a virgin's face;
Yet I was ever taught 'twas base to lie.   270
POLYDAMAS
You've been too bold, and you must love no more.
PALMYRA
Indeed I must; I cannot help my love;
I was so tender when I took the bent,
That now I grow that way.

247 *repartee* quick, witty reply
264 *gripe* not an alternative spelling for 'grip', but a separate word meaning 'clutch'
273 *took the bent* The image is of training a young plant to grow in a certain direction.

POLYDAMAS
  He is a prince; and you are meanly born.   275

LEONIDAS
  Love either finds equality, or makes it.
  Like death, he knows no difference in degrees,
  But planes and levels all.

PALMYRA
  Alas, I had not rendered up my heart,
  Had he not loved me first; but he preferred me   280
  Above the maidens of my age and rank,
  Still shunned their company and still sought mine.
  I was not won by gifts, yet still he gave;
  And all his gifts, though small, yet spoke his love.
  He picked the earliest strawberries in woods,   285
  The clustered filberts and the purple grapes.
  He taught a prating stare to speak my name,
  And when he found a nest of nightingales,
  Or callow linnets, he would show them me,
  And let me take them out.   290

POLYDAMAS
  This is a little mistress, meanly born,
  Fit only for a prince his vacant hours;
  And then, to laugh at her simplicity
  Not fix a passion there. Now hear my sentence.

LEONIDAS
  Remember, ere you give it, 'tis pronounced   295
  Against us both.

POLYDAMAS
  First, in her hand
  There shall be placed a player's painted sceptre,
  And on her head a gilded pageant crown;
  Thus shall she go,   300

---

286 *filberts* cultivated hazel nuts. There was perhaps felt to be something risible about
    this word; at any rate, Buckingham in *The Rehearsal* plays satirically with it (V.i.67).
287 *prating stare* chattering starling (not unusual in pre-budgie days: cf I Henry IV I.iii)
289 *callow* young, unfledged
297 *First...* In her last speech Palmyra has recalled the life of rustic simplicity with the
    description of which Act II ended. Perdita in *The Winter's Tale* IV.iv is the play
    queen at the sheep-shearing, a 'poor lowly maid, / Most goddess-like prank'd up',
    although she is in fact, like Palmyra, daughter of the king of Sicily. Polydamas
    makes Palmyra a play queen here and sentences her, not directly to death but to the
    likelihood of death, just as Perdita as a baby, at the end of Act II of *The Winter's
    Tale*, is sentenced not to be burnt but to be abandoned. There is no shame, of
    course, in Perdita's being a play queen, and the parallel in this instance is Palmyra's
    memory (at II.i.428) of being 'the lady of the May'.

With all the boys attending on her triumph.
That done, be put alone into a boat,
With bread and water only for three days,
So on the sea she shall be set adrift,
And who relieves her, dies.   305

PALMYRA
I only beg that you would execute
The last part first: let me be put to sea.
The bread and water, for my three days' life,
I give you back, I would not live so long.
But let me 'scape the shame.

LEONIDAS   Look to me, Piety;   310
And you, O Gods, look to my piety:
Keep me from saying that which misbecomes a son,
But let me die before I see this done.

POLYDAMAS
If you for ever will abjure her sight,
I can be yet a father; she shall live.   315

LEONIDAS
Hear, O you powers, is this to be a father?
I see 'tis all my happiness and quiet
You aim at, Sir; and take them.
I will not save even my Palmyra's life
At that ignoble price; but I'll die with her.   320

PALMYRA
So had I done by you,
Had fate made me a princess. Death, methinks,
Is not a terror now.
He is not fierce, or grim, but fawns and soothes me,
And slides along, like Cleopatra's aspic,   325
Offering his service to my troubled breast.

---

310 *Piety* This seems like a direct address to Palmyra, who is made the epitome of
    'piety', in that she responds dutifully to the claims of love for Leonidas. In the next
    lines Leonidas speaks of the conflicting duties between which he is set, to his love
    for Palmyra and to his father. Later in the play, Palmyra finds herself in precisely
    the same position.

313 *let me die* Leonidas uses with utmost seriousness words which we recall as a cant,
    meaningless phrase often in Melantha's mouth. The distance between love in the
    comic plot and love in the heroic plot is accurately fixed here.

325 *Cleopatra's aspic* at the end of *Antony and Cleopatra* which of course Dryden
    himself rewrote as *All for Love*)

LEONIDAS
   Begin what you have purposed when you please,
   Lead her to scorn, your triumph shall be doubled.
   As holy priests
   In pity go with dying malefactors	330
   So will I share her shame.
POLYDAMAS
   You shall not have your will so much; first part them,
   Then execute your office.
LEONIDAS (*draws his sword*) No; I'll die
   In her defence.
PALMYRA   Ah, hold, and pull not on
   A curse, to make me worthy of my death.	335
   Do not by lawless force oppose your father,
   Whom you have too much disobeyed for me.
LEONIDAS (*presenting his sword to his father upon his knees*)
   Here, take it, Sir, and with it pierce my heart:
   You have done more, in taking my Palmyra.
   You are my father, therefore I submit.	340
POLYDAMAS
   Keep him from anything he may design
   Against his life, whilst the first fury lasts;
   And now perform what I commanded you.
LEONIDAS
   In vain; if sword and poison be denied me,
   I'll hold my breath and die.	345
PALMYRA
   Farewell, my last Leonidas; yet live,
   I charge you live, till you believe me dead.
   I cannot die in peace if you die first.
   If life's a blessing, you shall have it last.
POLYDAMAS
   Go on with her, and lead him after me.	350

     Enter ARGALEON *hastily, with* HERMOGENES

ARGALEON
   I bring you, Sir, such news as must amaze you,
   And such as will prevent you from an action
   Which would have rendered all your life unhappy.

---

340 *I submit* He submits to his father's authority in offering his life, but he does not
    submit to his father's will that he should marry Amalthea.
346 *my last Leonidas* a piece of syntactic compression worthy of Shakespeare, the
    adjective perhaps signifying 'at last', or perhaps 'dying'

HERMOGENES *kneels*

POLYDAMAS
Hermogenes, you bend your knees in vain,
My doom's already past.   355
HERMOGENES
I kneel not for Palmyra, for I know
She will not need my prayers, but for myself;
With a feigned tale I have abused your ears,
And therefore merit death; but since, unforced,
I first accuse myself, I hope your mercy.   360
POLYDAMAS
Haste to explain your meaning.
HERMOGENES
Then, in few words, Palmyra is your daughter.
POLYDAMAS
How can I give belief to this impostor?
He who has once abused me, often may.
I'll hear no more.
ARGALEON   For your own sake, you must.   365
HERMOGENES
A parent's love (for I confess my crime)
Moved me to say Leonidas was yours;
But when I heard Palmyra was to die,
The fear of guiltless blood so stung my conscience,
That I resolved, even with my shame, to save   370
Your daughter's life.
POLYDAMAS
But how can I be certain, but that interest,
Which moved you first to say your son was mine,
Does not now move you too to save your daughter?
HERMOGENES
You had but then my word; I bring you now   375
Authentic testimonies. Sir, in short,

Delivers on his knees a jewel, and a letter

If this will not convince you, let me suffer.
POLYDAMAS (*looking first on the jewel*)
I know this jewel well; 'twas once my mother's,
Which, marrying, I presented to my wife.
And this, O this, is my Eudocia's hand.   380
(*reads*) *This was the pledge of love given to Eudocia,*
Who, dying, to her young Palmyra leaves it.

355 *doom* judgement

And this when you, my dearest Lord, receive,
Own her, and think on me, dying Eudocia,
(*to* ARGALEON) Take it; 'tis well there is no more to read,   385
My eyes grow full, and swim in their own light.

He embraces PALMYRA

PALMYRA
    I fear, Sir, this is your intended pageant.
    You sport yourself at poor Palmyra's cost;
    But if you think to make me proud,
    Indeed I cannot be so. I was born   390
    With humble thoughts, and lowly, like my birth.
    A real fortune could not make me haughty,
    Much less a feigned.
POLYDAMAS   This was her mother's temper.
    I have too much deserved thou shouldst suspect
    That I am not thy father; but my love   395
    Shall henceforth show I am. Behold my eyes,
    And see a father there begin to flow:
    This is not feigned, Palmyra.
PALMYRA
    I doubt no longer, Sir; you are a king,
    And cannot lie: falsehood's a vice too base   400
    To find a room in any royal breast.
    I know, in spite of my unworthiness,
    I am your child; for when you would have killed me,
    Methought I loved you then.
ARGALEON
    Sir, we forget the Prince Leonidas,   405
    His greatness should not stand neglected thus.
POLYDAMAS
    Guards, you may now retire. Give him his sword,
    And leave him free.
                                              [*Exeunt guards*]
LEONIDAS
    Then the first use I make of liberty
    Shall be, with your permission, mighty Sir,   410
    To pay that reverence to which nature binds me.

Kneels to HERMOGENES

387 *pageant* See III. i. 299.
393 *temper* temperament
411 *To...me* Leonidas' oscillating fortunes are parodied in the character of Prince
     Pretty-man in *The Rehearsal:* 'Sometimes a Fishers Son, sometimes a Prince'
     (III. iv. 59).

ARGALEON
   Sure you forget your birth, thus to misplace
   This act of your obedience; you should kneel
   To nothing but to heaven, and to a king.

LEONIDAS
   I never shall forget what nature owes,   415
   Nor be ashamed to pay it; though my father
   Be not a king, I know him brave and honest,
   And well deserving of a worthier son.

POLYDAMAS
   He bears it gallantly.

LEONIDAS (*to* HERMOGENES)
   Why would you not instruct me, Sir, before,   420
   Where I should place my duty?
   From which, if ignorance have made me swerve,
   I beg your pardon for an erring son.

PALMYRA
   I almost grieve I am a princess, since
   It makes him lose a crown.   425

LEONIDAS [*kneeling to the king*]
   And next, to you my King, thus low I kneel
   To implore your mercy. If in that small time
   I had the honour to be thought your son,
   I paid not strict obedience to your will.
   I thought, indeed, I should not be compelled,   430
   But thought it as your son; so what I took
   In duty from you, I restored in courage,
   Because your son should not be forced.

POLYDAMAS
   You have my pardon for it.

LEONIDAS
   To you, fair Princess, I congratulate   435
   Your birth, of which I ever thought you worthy.
   And give me leave to add, that I am proud
   The gods have picked me out to be the man
   By whose dejected fate yours is to rise;
   Because no man could more desire your fortune,   440
   Or franklier part with his to make you great.

PALMYRA
   I know the king, though you are not his son,

430 *should not* ought not to

Will still regard you as my foster-brother,
And so conduct you downward from a throne
By slow degrees, so unperceived and soft,   445
That it may seem no fall; or, if it be,
May fortune lay a bed of down beneath you.

POLYDAMAS
He shall be ranked with my nobility,
And kept from scorn by a large pension given him.

LEONIDAS (*bowing*)
You are all great and royal in your gifts,   450
But at the donor's feet I lay them down.
Should I take riches from you, it would seem
As I did want a soul to bear that poverty
To which the gods designed my humble birth.
And should I take your honours without merit,   455
It would appear I wanted manly courage
To hope them, in your service, from my sword.

POLYDAMAS
Still brave, and like yourself.
The court shall shine this night in its full splendour,
And celebrate this new discovery.   460
Argaleon, lead my daughter: as we go,
I shall have time to give her my commands,
In which you are concerned.

Exeunt all but LEONIDAS

LEONIDAS
Methinks I do not want
That huge long train of fawning followers   465
That swept a furlong after me.
'Tis true, I am alone;
So was the Godhead ere he made the world,
And better served Himself than served by nature.
And yet I have a soul   470
Above this humble fate. I could command,

---

449 *large pension* So immediate and unvarnished a connection between honour and
money must surely have been half-humorous (though probably only half) on
Dryden's part, and must always have made the audience laugh.

462–3 *I shall...concerned* The spectacle of a king trying a second time, after one near
disaster, to impose his marriage will reminds us of the end of *All's Well That Ends
Well*, where the king of France offers the virgin Diana any young man she chooses,
even though such an offer to Helena at the beginning of the play was the cause of all
the trouble.

471 *humble fate* Humble it may be, but it has allowed a fairly extravagant comparison
with the godhead three lines earlier.

Love to do good, give largely to true merit;
All that a king should do. But though these are not
My province, I have scene enough within
To exercise my virtue.   475
All that a heart so fixed as mine can move
Is, that my niggard fortune starves my love.

                                                            Exit

Act III, Scene ii

PALAMEDE *and* DORALICE *meet: she, with a book in her hand,*
           seems to start at the sight of him

DORALICE
'Tis a strange thing that no warning will serve your turn;
and that no retirement will secure me from your impertinent
addresses! Did not I tell you that I was to be private here at
my devotions?
PALAMEDE
Yes; and you see I have observed my cue exactly. I am come   5
to relieve you from them. Come, shut up, shut up your
book; the man's come who is to supply all your necessities.
DORALICE
Then, it seems, you are so impudent to think it was an assignation? This, I warrant, was your lewd interpretation of
my innocent meaning.   10
PALAMEDE
Venus forbid that I should harbour so unreasonable a
thought of a fair young lady, that you should lead me hither
into temptation. I confess I might think indeed it was a
kind of honourable challenge, to meet privately without
seconds, and decide the difference betwixt the two sexes;   15
but heaven forgive me if I thought amiss.
DORALICE
You thought too, I'll lay my life on't, that you might as
well make love to me, as my husband does to your mistress.
PALAMEDE
I was so unreasonable to think so too.
DORALICE
And then you wickedly inferred, that there was some   20
justice in the revenge of it, or at least but little injury, for a

474 *scene* territory, scope
12–13 *lead...temptation* an echo, of course, of the Lord's Prayer

man to endeavour to enjoy that which he accounts a blessing
and which is not valued as it ought by the dull possessor.
Confess your wickedness. Did you not think so?

PALAMEDE

I confess I was thinking so, as fast as I could; but you think   25
so much before me that you will let me think nothing.

DORALICE

'Tis the very thing that I designed. I have forestalled all
your arguments, and left you without a word more, to
plead for mercy. If you have anything farther to offer, ere
sentence pass – poor animal, I brought you hither only for   30
my diversion.

PALAMEDE

That you may have, if you'll make use of me the right way;
but I tell thee, woman, I am now past talking.

DORALICE

But it may be I came hither to hear what fine things you
could say for yourself.   35

PALAMEDE

You would be very angry, to my knowledge, if I should
lose so much time to say many of them – by this hand you
would –

DORALICE

Fie, Palamede, I am a woman of honour.

PALAMEDE

I see you are; you have kept touch with your assignation;   40
and before we part you shall find that I am a man of honour
– yet I have one scruple of conscience –

DORALICE

I warrant you will not want some naughty argument or
other to satisfy yourself – I hope you are afraid of betraying
your friend?   45

PALAMEDE

Of betraying my friend! I am more afraid of being betrayed
by you to my friend. You women now are got into the way
of telling first yourselves. A man who has any care of his
reputation will be loath to trust it with you.

DORALICE

O, you charge your faults upon our sex. You men are like   50
cocks; you never make love but you clap your wings and
crow when you have done.

---

51 *cocks* In the mediaeval account and elsewhere, the cock is described as the most
   lustful of all animals because he crows aloud after copulating instead of sinking, like
   all others, into post-coital gloom.

PALAMEDE
    Nay, rather you women are like hens; you never lay but
    you cackle an hour after, to discover your nest – but I'll
    venture it for once.   55
DORALICE
    To convince you that you are in the wrong, I'll retire into
    the dark grotto, to my devotion, and make so little noise
    that it shall be impossible for you to find me.
PALAMEDE
    But if I find you –
DORALICE
    Ay, if you find me – but I'll put you to search in more   60
    corners than you imagine.

                        She runs in, and he after her

                Enter RHODOPHIL *and* MELANTHA

MELANTHA
    Let me die but this solitude and that grotto are scandalous.
    I'll go no further; besides, you have a sweet lady of your own.
RHODOPHIL
    But a sweet mistress, now and then, makes my sweet lady
    so much more sweet.   65
MELANTHA
    I hope you will not force me?
RHODOPHIL
    But I will, if you desire it.
PALAMEDE (*within*)
    Where the devil are you, Madam? 'Sdeath, I begin to be
    weary of this hide and seek. If you stay a little longer, till the
    fit's over, I'll hide in my turn and put you to the finding me. 70

            He enters, and sees RHODOPHIL *and* MELANTHA

    [*aside*] How! Rhodophil and my mistress!
MELANTHA [*aside*]
    My servant to apprehend me! This is *surprenant au dernier*.
RHODOPHIL [*aside*]
    I must on; there's nothing but impudence can help me out.
PALAMEDE
    Rhodophil! How came you hither in so good company?
RHODOPHIL
    As you see, Palamede, an effect of pure friendship. I was   75
    not able to live without you.

    60–1 *more corners* not only corners of the grotto but of her body
    70 *fit* Palamede's sexual arousal
    72 *surprenant au dernier* in the highest degree surprising

PALAMEDE
  But what makes my mistress with you?

RHODOPHIL
  Why, I heard you were here alone, and could not in civility
  but bring her to you.

MELANTHA
  You'll pardon the effects of a passion which I may now avow   80
  for you, if it transported me beyond the rules of *bienséance*.

PALAMEDE
  But who told you I was here? They that told you that may
  tell you more, for aught I know.

RHODOPHIL
  O, for that matter, we had intelligence.

PALAMEDE
  But let me tell you, we came hither so very privately that   85
  you could not trace us.

RHODOPHIL
  Us? What us? You are alone.

PALAMEDE
  Us! [*aside*] The devil's in me for mistaking: [*to him*] me, I
  meant. Or us; that is, you are me, or I you, as we are
  friends: that's us.   90

DORALICE (*within*)
  Palamede, Palamede.

RHODOPHIL
  I should know that voice? Who's within there, that calls you?

PALAMEDE
  Faith I can't imagine. I believe the place is haunted.

DORALICE (*within*)
  Palamede, Palamede. All-cocks hidden.

PALAMEDE [*aside*]
  Lord, lord, what shall I do? [*to him*] Well, dear friend, to   95
  let you see I scorn to be jealous, and that I dare trust my
  mistress with you, take her back; for I would not willingly
  have her frighted, and I am resolved to see who's there. I'll
  not be daunted with a bugbear, that's certain. Prithee
  dispute it not, it shall be so. Nay, do not put me to swear,   100
  but go quickly. There's an effect of pure friendship for
  you now.

Enter DORALICE *and looks amazed, seeing them*

81 *bienséance* decency, decorum
94 *All-cocks hidden* The children's cry of 'all hidden' in hide and seek. Doralice has
   also already mentioned cocks at III.ii. 51, and there is clearly a sexual innuendo.
99 *bugbear* hobgoblin

RHODOPHIL
Doralice! I am thunderstruck to see you here.

PALAMEDE
So am I! Quite thunderstruck. Was it you that called me
within? [*aside*] I must be impudent.   105

RHODOPHIL
How came you hither, spouse?

PALAMEDE
Ay, how came you hither? And, which is more, how could
you be here without my knowledge?

DORALICE (*to her husband*)
O, gentleman, have I caught you i'faith! Have I broke forth
in ambush upon you! I thought my suspicions would prove   110
true.

RHODOPHIL
Suspicions! This is very fine, spouse! Prithee what
suspicions?

DORALICE
O, you feign ignorance. Why, of you and Melantha. Here
have I stayed these two hours, waiting with all the rage of a   115
passionate, loving wife, but infinitely jealous, to take you
two in the manner. For hither I was certain you would
come.

RHODOPHIL
But you are mistaken, spouse, in the occasion; for we came
hither on purpose to find Palamede, on intelligence he was   120
gone before.

PALAMEDE
I'll be hanged, then, if the same party who gave you
intelligence I was here, did not tell your wife you would
come hither. Now I smell the malice on't on both sides.

DORALICE
Was it so, think you? Nay, then, I'll confess my part of the   125
malice too. As soon as ever I spied my husband and
Melantha come together, I had a strange temptation to
make him jealous in revenge; and that made me call
Palamede, Palamede, as though there had been an intrigue
between us.   130

MELANTHA
Nay, I avow, there was an appearance of an intrigue
between us too.

112–13 *printed as two lines of verse in Q1*

117 *manner* act

PALAMEDE
  To see how things will come about!
RHODOPHIL (*embraces*)
  And was it only thus, my dear Doralice?
DORALICE (*embracing him*)
  And did I wrong n'own, Rhodophil, with a false suspicion?   135
PALAMEDE (*aside*)
  Now am I confident we had all four the same design. 'Tis a
  pretty odd kind of game this, where each of us plays for
  double stakes. This is just thrust and parry with the same
  motion. I am to get his wife, and yet to guard my own
  mistress. But I am vilely suspicious that, while I conquer in   140
  the right wing, I shall be routed in the left; for both our
  women will certainly betray their party, because they are
  each of them for gaining of two, as well as we; and I much
  fear:
  If their necessities and ours were known,   145
  They have more need of two, than we of one.
                                Exeunt, embracing one another

Act IV, Scene i

Enter LEONIDAS *musing;* AMALTHEA *following him*

AMALTHEA
  Yonder he is, and I must speak, or die;
  And yet 'tis death to speak; yet he must know
  I have a passion for him, and may know it
  With a less blush, because to offer it
  To his low fortunes shows I loved before   5
  His person, not his greatness.
LEONIDAS
  First scorned, and now commanded from the court!
  The king is good, but he is wrought to this
  By proud Argaleon's malice.
  What more disgrace can love and fortune join   10
  To inflict upon one man? I cannot now

---

135 *n'own* D (none Q1)

---

135 *n'own* mine own
138–9 *thrust...motion* each one accusing the other of the offence he defends himself
     against
146 *need* sexual need

Behold my dear Palmyra; she, perhaps, too
Is grown ashamed of a mean ill-placed love.
AMALTHEA (*aside*)
  Assist me, Venus, for I tremble when
  I am to speak, but I must force myself.   15
  (*to him*) Sir, I would crave but one short minute with you,
  And some few words.
LEONIDAS (*aside*)   The proud Argaleon's sister!
AMALTHEA (*aside*)
  Alas, it will not out; shame stops my mouth.
  [*to him*] Pardon my error, Sir, I was mistaken,
  And took you for another.   20
LEONIDAS (*aside*)
  In spite of all his guards, I'll see Palmyra;
  Though meanly born, I have a kingly soul yet.
AMALTHEA (*aside*)
  I stand upon a precipice, where fain
  I would retire, but love still thrusts me on:
  Now I grow bolder, and will speak to him.   25
  (*to him*) Sir, 'tis indeed to you that I would speak,
  And if –
LEONIDAS   O, you are sent to scorn my fortunes.
  Your sex and beauty are your privilege;
  But should your brother –
AMALTHEA [*aside*]
  Now he looks angry, and I dare not speak.   30
  [*to him*] I had some business with you, Sir,
  But 'tis not worth your knowledge.
LEONIDAS
  Then 'twill be charity to let me mourn
  My griefs alone, for I am much disordered.
AMALTHEA
  'Twill be more charity to mourn them with you: 35
  Heaven knows I pity you.
LEONIDAS   Your pity, Madam,
  Is generous, but 'tis unavailable.
AMALTHEA
  You know not till 'tis tried.
  Your sorrows are no secret; you have lost
  A crown, and mistress.
LEONIDAS   Are not these enough?   40
  Hang two such weights on any other soul,
  And see if it can bear them.

37 *unavailable* unavailing

AMALTHEA
  More; you are banished by my brother's means,
  And ne'er must hope again to see your princess,
  Except as prisoners view fair walks and streets,   45
  And careless passengers, going by their grates,
  To make them feel the want of liberty.
  But, worse than all,
  The king this morning has enjoined his daughter
  To accept my brother's love.
LEONIDAS   Is this your pity?   50
  You aggravate my griefs and print them deeper
  In new and heavier stamps.
AMALTHEA
  'Tis as physicians show the desperate ill
  To endear their art, by mitigating pains
  They cannot wholly cure. When you despair   55
  Of all you wish, some part of it, because
  Unhoped for, may be grateful; and some other –
LEONIDAS
  What other?
AMALTHEA
  Some other may –
  (aside) My shame again has seized me, and I can go   60
  No farther –
LEONIDAS
  These often failings, sighs, and interruptions,
  Make me imagine you have grief like mine.
  Have you ne'er loved?
AMALTHEA   I? Never. (aside) 'Tis in vain;
  I must despair in silence.   65
LEONIDAS
  You come as I suspected then, to mock.
  At least observe my griefs; take it not ill
  That I must leave you.
                          Is going
AMALTHEA
  You must not go with these unjust opinions.
  Command my life and fortunes; you are wise,   70

62 *failings* Q3 (failing Q1)
66 *mock.* (mock, Q1)

---

46 *passengers* passers by
  grates barred prison windows
57 *grateful* welcome, pleasing
67 *observe* take note of

Think, and think well, what I can do to serve you.

LEONIDAS
I have but one thing in my thoughts and wishes.
If by your means I can obtain the sight
Of my adored Palmyra; or, what's harder,
One minute's time, to tell her I die hers.   75

She starts back

I see I am not to expect it from you;
Nor could, indeed, with reason.

AMALTHEA
Name any other thing. Is Amalthea
So despicable, she can serve your wishes
In this alone?

LEONIDAS   If I should ask of heaven,   80
I have no other suit.

AMALTHEA
To show you, then, I can deny you nothing,
Though 'tis more hard to me than any other,
Yet I will do it for you.

LEONIDAS
Name quickly, name the means, speak, my good angel.   85

AMALTHEA
Be not so much o'erjoyed; for if you are,
I'll rather die than do it. This night the court
Will be in masquerade.
You shall attend on me; in that disguise
You may both see and speak to her,   90
If you dare venture it.

LEONIDAS
Yes, were a god her guardian,
And bore in each hand thunder, I would venture.

AMALTHEA
Farewell then; two hours hence I will expect you.
My heart's so full that I can stay no longer.   95

Exit

LEONIDAS
Already it grows dusky. I'll prepare
With haste for my disguise. But who are these?

Enter HERMOGENES *and* EUBULUS

HERMOGENES
'Tis he; we need not fear to speak to him.

EUBULUS
Leonidas.

LEONIDAS   Sure I have known that voice.
HERMOGENES
    You have some reason, Sir; 'tis Eubulus,   100
    Who bred you with the princess; and, departing,
    Bequeathed you to my care.
LEONIDAS (*kneeling*)
    My foster-father! Let my knees express
    My joys for your return!
EUBULUS
    Rise, Sir, you must not kneel.
LEONIDAS   E'er since you left me,   105
    I have been wandering in a maze of fate,
    Led by false fires of a fantastic glory,
    And the vain lustre of imagined crowns.
    But ah! Why would you leave me? Or how could you
    Absent yourself so long?   110
EUBULUS
    I'll give you a most just account of both;
    And something more I have to tell you, which
    I know must cause your wonder; but this place,
    Though almost hid in darkness, is not safe.

                    Torches appear

    Already I discern some coming towards us   115
    With lights, who may discover me. Hermogenes,
    Your lodgings are hard by, and much more private.
HERMOGENES
    There you may freely speak.
LEONIDAS   Let us make haste;
    For some affairs, and of no small importance,
    Call me another way.   120
                                 Exeunt

Enter PALAMEDE *and* RHODOPHIL *with vizor masks in their
           hands and torches before them*

PALAMEDE
    We shall have noble sport tonight, Rhodophil; this
    masquerading is a most glorious invention.
RHODOPHIL
    I believe it was invented first by some jealous lover, to

---

103 *foster-father* Q4 (Foster, Father Q1)

120+ *vizor masks* face masks

discover the haunts of his jilting mistress; or perhaps by
some distressed servant, to gain an opportunity with a   125
jealous man's wife.

PALAMEDE
No, it must be the invention of a woman; it has so much of
subtlety and love in it.

RHODOPHIL
I am sure 'tis extremely pleasant, for to go unknown is the
next degree to going invisible.   130

PALAMEDE
What with our antique habits and feigned voices, do you
know me? And I know you? Methinks we move and talk
just like so many overgrown puppets.

RHODOPHIL
Masquerade is only vizor-mask improved, a heightening of
the same fashion.   135

PALAMEDE
No. Masquerade is vizor-mask in debauch, and I like it the
better for it. For, with a vizor-mask we fool ourselves into
courtship for the sake of an eye that glanced, or a hand that
stole itself out of the glove sometimes, to give us a sample of
the skin. But in masquerade there is nothing to be known,   140
she's all *terra incognita*, and the bold discoverer leaps
ashore and takes his lot among the wild Indians and savages,
without the vile consideration of safety to his person, or of
beauty or wholesomeness in his mistress.

Enter BELIZA

RHODOPHIL
Beliza, what make you here?   145

BELIZA
Sir, my lady sent me after you, to let you know she finds
herself a little indisposed, so that she cannot be at court,
but is retired to rest in her own apartment, where she shall
want the happiness of your dear embraces tonight.

124 *jilting* deceiving
134 *Masquerade...improved* Masquerade involved not only face masks but costume
    disguise as well. At Prologue 4, the habit of prostitutes of wearing masks is alluded
    to.
141 *terra incognita* unknown territory
145 *make you* are you doing
149 *want* In the surface sense, 'desire', but the clear underlying sense, taken up
    immediately by Rhodophil, is 'lack'.

RHODOPHIL
A very fine phrase, Beliza, to let me know my wife desires   150
to lie alone.

PALAMEDE
I doubt, Rhodophil, you take the pains sometimes to
instruct your wife's woman in these elegancies.

RHODOPHIL
Tell my dear lady, that since I must be so unhappy as not to
wait on her tonight, I will lament bitterly for her absence.   155
'Tis true I shall be at court, but I will take no divertisement
there; and when I return to my solitary bed, if I am so
forgetful of my passion as to sleep, I will dream of her; and
betwixt sleep and waking put out my foot towards her side
for midnight consolation; and not finding her, I will sigh,   160
and imagine myself a most desolate widower.

BELIZA
I shall do your commands, Sir.

Exit

RHODOPHIL (*aside*)
She's sick as aptly for my purpose as if she had contrived it
so. Well, if ever woman was a help-meet for man, my spouse
is so; for within this hour I received a note from Melantha,   165
that she would meet me this evening in masquerade in boy's
habit, to rejoice with me before she entered into fetters. For
I find she loves me better than Palamede only because he's
to be her husband. There's something of antipathy in the
word marriage to the nature of love; marriage is the mere   170
ladle of affection, that cools it when 'tis never so fiercely
boiling over.

PALAMEDE
Dear Rhodophil, I must needs beg your pardon. There is
an occasion fallen out which I had forgot. I cannot be at
court tonight.   175

RHODOPHIL
Dear Palamede, I am sorry we shall not have one course

---

152 *doubt* suspect
164 *help-meet* helpmate. I have not modernised this spelling, because the word as it
stands in Q1, as often used in the seventeenth century, derives directly from the text
of the King James Bible: 'I will make him an help meet for him' (Genesis 2: 18). The
word arises from a mistaken putting together of noun and adjective in the original
text to form a single noun.
176 *course* a hunting term for 'run, gallop at the prey'

together at the herd; but I find your game lies single. Good
fortune to you with your mistress.

Exit

PALAMEDE
He has wished me good fortune with his wife. There's no sin
in this then, there's fair leave given. Well, I must go visit   180
the sick; I cannot resist the temptations of my charity. O
what a difference will she find betwixt a dull resty husband
and a quick vigorous lover! He sets out like a carrier's horse,
plodding on because he knows he must, with the bells of
matrimony chiming so melancholy about his neck, in pain   185
till he's at his journey's end; and despairing to get thither,
he is fain to fortify imagination with the thoughts of another
woman. I take heat after heat, like a well-breathed courser,
and – but hark, what noise is that? Swords!

Clashing of swords within

Nay, then have with you.   *Exit* PALAMEDE   190

Re-enter PALAMEDE *with* RHODOPHIL, *and*
DORALICE *in man's habit*

RHODOPHIL
Friend, your relief was very timely, otherwise I had been
oppressed.
PALAMEDE
What was the quarrel?
RHODOPHIL
What I did was in rescue of this youth.
PALAMEDE
What cause could he give them?   195
DORALICE
The cause was nothing but only the common cause of
fighting in masquerades: they were drunk, and I was sober.
RHODOPHIL
Have they not hurt you?
DORALICE
No; but I am exceeding ill with the fright on't.

188 *I* Q2 (I, Q1)

---

177 *game lies single* Hunting terminology again; but it is indeed also the case that
    Palamede's game is to be with Doralice, who waits alone for him.
182 *resty* sluggish   183 *quick* lively
188 *heat after heat* The word 'heat' is used of a run given to a racehorse. Palamede
    clearly intends to suggest that he can couple again and again with Doralice without
    tiring.

PALAMEDE
  Let's lead him to some place where he may refresh himself.   200
RHODOPHIL
  Do you conduct him then.
PALAMEDE (*aside*)
  How cross this happens to my design of going to Doralice!
  For I am confident she was sick on purpose that I should
  visit her. Hark you, Rhodophil, could not you take care of
  the stripling? I am partly engaged tonight.   205
RHODOPHIL
  You know I have business. But come, youth, if it must be so.
DORALICE (*to* RHODOPHIL)
  No, good Sir, do not give yourself that trouble; I shall be
  safer and better pleased with your friend here.
RHODOPHIL
  Farewell then; once more I wish you a good adventure.
PALAMEDE
  Damn this kindness! Now must I be troubled with this   210
  young rogue, and miss my opportunity with Doralice.
        Exit RHODOPHIL *alone*, PALAMEDE *with* DORALICE

Act IV, Scene ii

Enter POLYDAMAS

POLYDAMAS
  Argaleon counselled well to banish him.
  He has I know not what
  Of greatness in his looks, and of high fate,
  That almost awes me; but I fear my daughter,
  Who hourly moves me for him, and I marked   5
  She sighed when I but named Argaleon to her.
  But see, the masquers: hence my cares, this night,
  At least take truce and find me on my pillow.

Enter [PALMYRA] *the princess in masquerade, with ladies: at the
  other end* ARGALEON *and gentlemen in masquerade: then*
  LEONIDAS *leading* AMALTHEA. *The king sits.*
  A dance. After the dance

AMALTHEA (*to* LEONIDAS)
  That's the princess;

---

5 *moves* beseeches
9 *That's the princess* The masked scene between the lovers recalls the first meeting of
  Romeo and Juliet at the Capulets' ball.

I saw the habit ere she put it on.   10
LEONIDAS
I know her by a thousand other signs,
She cannot hide so much divinity.
Disguised, and silent, yet some graceful motion
Breaks from her, and shines round her like a glory.

Goes to PALMYRA

AMALTHEA
Thus she reveals herself, and knows it not.   15
Like love's dark-lantern I direct his steps,
And yet he sees not that which gives him light.
PALMYRA (*to* LEONIDAS)
I know you; but alas, Leonidas,
Why should you tempt this danger on yourself?
LEONIDAS
Madam, you know me not if you believe   20
I would not hazard greater for your sake:
But you, I fear, are changed.
PALMYRA
No, I am still the same;
But there are many things became Palmyra
Which ill become the princess.
LEONIDAS   I ask nothing   25
Which honour will not give you leave to grant:
One hour's short audience, at my father's house,
You cannot sure refuse me.
PALMYRA
Perhaps I should, did I consult strict virtue;
But something must be given to love and you.   30
When would you I should come?
LEONIDAS
This evening, with the speediest opportunity.
I have a secret to discover to you,
Which will surprise and please you.
PALMYRA   'Tis enough.
Go now; for we may be observed and known.   35
I trust your honour; give me not occasion
To blame myself, or you.
LEONIDAS
You never shall repent your good opinion.
Kisses her hand and exit

16 *dark-lantern* A lantern with a slide by which the light can be concealed partially or
   wholly. Here the light, as it were, is partly concealed, to guide the stealthy footsteps
   of a lover.

ARGALEON [*aside*]
  I cannot be deceived; that is the princess;
  One of her maids betrayed the habit to me.   40
  But who was he with whom she held discourse?
  'Tis one she favours, for he kissed her hand.
  Our shapes are like, our habits near the same:
  She may mistake, and speak to me for him.
  I am resolved, I'll satisfy my doubts,   45
  Though to be more tormented.

                                                    Exit

              [*A song is sung*]

                        1.

  Whilst Alexis lay pressed
  In her arms he loved best,
  With his hands round her neck, and his head on her breast,
  He found the fierce pleasure too hasty to stay,   50
  And his soul in the tempest just flying away.

                        2.

  When Celia saw this,
  With a sigh, and a kiss,
  She cried, Oh my dear, I am robbed of my bliss;
  'Tis unkind to your love, and unfaithfully done,   55
  To leave me behind you, and die all alone.

                        3.

  The youth, though in haste,
  And breathing his last,
  In pity died slowly, while she died more fast;
  Till at length she cried, Now my dear, now let us go,   60
  Now die, my Alexis, and I will die too.

                        4.

  Thus entranced they did lie,
  Till Alexis did try
  To recover new breath, that again he might die:
  Then often they died, but the more they did so,   65
  The nymph died more quick, and the shepherd more slow.

47 *Whilst Alexis...* The song was set to music by Nicholas Staggins (?1650–1700), in
   the triple time popular in the 1670s.
50 *too hasty to stay* He was so excited that he began to lose control and ejaculate.
54 *robbed of my bliss* Because she wanted to copulate longer until she too came to
   orgasm.
56 *die* ejaculate, come to orgasm. The pun with the other meaning of 'die' was
   extremely common in the seventeenth century.

Another dance. After it ARGALEON *re-enters, and stands
by the princess*

PALMYRA (*to* ARGALEON)
Leonidas, what means this quick return?
ARGALEON [*aside*]
O heaven! 'Tis what I feared.
PALMYRA
Is aught of moment happened since you went?
ARGALEON
No, Madam, but I understood not fully   70
Your last commands.
PALMYRA   And yet you answered to them.
Retire; you are too indiscreet a lover.
I'll meet you where I promised.
                                        Exit

ARGALEON
O my cursed fortune! What have I discovered?
But I will be revenged.   75

Whispers to the king

POLYDAMAS
But are you certain you are not deceived?
ARGALEON
Upon my life.
POLYDAMAS   Her honour is concerned.
Somewhat I'll do; but I am yet distracted,
And know not where to fix. I wished a child,
And heaven, in anger, granted my request.   80
So blind we are, our wishes are so vain,
That what we most desire, proves most our pain.
                                        Exeunt omnes

Act IV, Scene iii

An eating-house; bottles of wine on the table; PALAMEDE,
and DORALICE *in man's habit*

DORALICE (*aside*)
Now cannot I find in my heart to discover myself, though I
long he should know me.
PALAMEDE
I tell thee, boy, now I have seen thee safe, I must be gone.
I have no leisure to throw away on thy raw conversation; I

am a person that understands better things, I.   5
DORALICE
Were I a woman, Oh how you'd admire me! Cry up every
word I said, and screw your face into a submissive smile;
as I have seen a dull gallant act wit and counterfeit pleasant-
ness, when he whispers to a great person in a playhouse.
Smile, and look briskly, when the other answers, as if some-   10
thing of extraordinary had passed betwixt them, when,
heaven knows, there was nothing else but: what o'clock
does your Lordship think it is? And my Lord's *repartee* is:
'tis almost park-time; or, at most: shall we out of the pit
and go behind the scenes for an act or two? And yet such   15
fine things as these would be wit in a mistress's mouth.
PALAMEDE
Ay, boy; there's Dame Nature in the case. He who cannot
find wit in a mistress deserves to find nothing else, boy.
But these are riddles to thee, child, and I have not leisure to
instruct thee. I have great affairs to dispatch, great affairs;   20
I am a man of business.
DORALICE
Come, you shall not go. You have no affairs but what you
may dispatch here, to my knowledge.
PALAMEDE
I find now, thou art a boy of more understanding than I
thought thee, a very lewd wicked boy. O' my conscience,   25
thou wouldst debauch me, and hast some evil designs upon
my person.
DORALICE
You are mistaken, Sir. I would only have you show me a
more lawful reason why you would leave me, than I can
why you should not, and I'll not stay you; for I am not so   30
young but I understand the necessities of flesh and blood,
and the pressing occasions of mankind, as well as you.
PALAMEDE
A very forward and understanding boy! Thou art in great
danger of a page's wit: to be brisk at fourteen, and dull at
twenty. But I'll give thee no further account; I must and   35
will go.

5 *understands* D (understand Q1)

---

10 *briskly* wittily, alertly
14 *park-time* time to walk in the park
26 *debauch me* Palamede thinks the boy is offering himself for sex.
30 *stay* keep

DORALICE
  My life on't, your mistress is not at home.
PALAMEDE [*aside*]
  This imp will make me very angry. [*to the boy*] I tell thee,
  young Sir, she is at home, and at home for me; and, which
  is more, she is abed for me, and sick for me.   40
DORALICE
  For you only?
PALAMEDE
  Ay, for me only.
DORALICE
  But how do you know she's sick abed?
PALAMEDE
  She sent her husband word so.
DORALICE
  And are you such a novice in love to believe a wife's   45
  message to her husband?
PALAMEDE
  Why, what the devil should be her meaning else?
DORALICE
  It may be, to go in masquerade as well as you, to observe
  your haunts and keep you company without your knowledge.
PALAMEDE
  Nay, I'll trust her for that. She loves me too well to disguise 50
  herself from me.
DORALICE
  If I were she, I would disguise on purpose to try your wit;
  and come to my servant like a riddle, read me, and take me.
PALAMEDE
  I could know her in any shape. My good genius would
  prompt me to find out a handsome woman. There's some-   55
  thing in her that would attract me to her without my
  knowledge.
DORALICE
  Then you make a loadstone of your mistress?
PALAMEDE
  Yes, and I carry steel about me which has been so often
  touched, that it never fails to point to the north pole.   60

---

53 *riddle, read me...me* Behind the common phrase 'riddle me ree' is this wording: that
    is, 'I am a riddle, understand me and take me to heart'. The sexual innuendo of
    'take me' is clear.
59 *steel* Steel is magnetised to point north by being touched by a magnet; 'steel' can
    also mean a sword. The metaphor is for Palamede's penis.

DORALICE
　Yet still my mind gives me, that you have met her dis-
guised tonight and have not known her.
PALAMEDE [*aside*]
　This is the most pragmatical conceited little fellow; he will
needs understand my business better than myself. [*to the
boy*] I tell thee, once more, thou dost not know my　　65
mistress.
DORALICE
　And I tell you, once more, that I know her better than you
do.
PALAMEDE [*aside*]
　The boy's resolved to have the last word. [*to the boy*] I find
I must go without reply.　　　　　　　　　　　　　　70
　　　　　　　　　　　　　　　　　　　　　Exit

DORALICE
　Ah mischief, I have lost him with my fooling. Palamede,
Palamede.

*He returns; she plucks off her peruke, and puts it on again when
he knows her*

PALAMEDE
　O heavens! Is it you, Madam?
DORALICE
　Now, where was your good genius, that would prompt you
to find me out?　　　　　　　　　　　　　　　　　75
PALAMEDE
　Why, you see I was not deceived; you yourself were my
good genius.
DORALICE
　But where was the steel that knew the loadstone? Ha?
PALAMEDE
　The truth is, Madam, the steel has lost its virtue; and
therefore, if you please, we'll new touch it.　　　　80

　　Enter RHODOPHIL, *and* MELANTHA *in boy's habit;*
　　RHODOPHIL *sees* PALAMEDE *kissing* DORALICE's *hand*

RHODOPHIL
　Palamede again! Am I fallen into your quarters? What?
Engaging with a boy? Is all honourable?
PALAMEDE
　O, very honourable on my side. I was just chastising this

61 *gives me* suggests to me
63 *pragmatical* meddlestome　　79 *virtue* magnetic strength

young villain; he was running away without paying his
share of the reckoning.   85

RHODOPHIL
Then I find I was deceived in him.

PALAMEDE
Yes, you are deceived in him. 'Tis the archest rogue, if you
did but know him.

MELANTHA [*to* RHODOPHIL]
Good Rhodophil, let us get off *à la dérobée*, for fear I should
be discovered.   90

RHODOPHIL [*to* MELANTHA]
There's no retiring now; I warrant you for discovery.
Now have I the oddest thought, to entertain you before
your servant's face, and he never the wiser. 'Twill be the
prettiest juggling trick to cheat him when he looks upon
us.   95

MELANTHA [*to* RHODOPHIL]
This is the strangest *caprice* in you.

PALAMEDE (*to* DORALICE)
This Rhodophil's the unluckiest fellow to me! This is now
the second time he has barred the dice when we were just
ready to have nicked him. But if ever I get the box again –

DORALICE [*to* PALAMEDE]
Do you think he will not know me? Am I like myself?   100

PALAMEDE [*to* DORALICE]
No more than a picture in the hangings.

DORALICE [*to* PALAMEDE]
Nay, then he can never discover me, now the wrong side of
the arras is turned towards him.

PALAMEDE [*to* DORALICE]
At least 'twill be some pleasure to me to enjoy what freedom
I can while he looks on. I will storm the outworks of   105
matrimony even before his face.

RHODOPHIL
What wine have you there, Palamede?

89 *à la* Q3 (*al-a* Q1)

---

87 *archest* most mischievous
91 *I warrant...discovery* I assure you you will not be discovered
96 *caprice* whim, fancy
98 *barred* voided, annulled the throw of
99 *nicked* scored against
   box The dice were shaken in a box, and it was the boxkeeper who gave each player
   his turn.
101 *picture...hangings* Figures woven in hanging tapestries were not very lifelike.

PALAMEDE
  Old Chios, or the rogue's damned that drew it.
RHODOPHIL
  Come: to the most constant of mistresses; that I believe is
  yours, Palamede.   110
DORALICE
  Pray spare your seconds; for my part I am but a weak brother.
PALAMEDE
  Now: to the truest of turtles; that is your wife, Rhodophil,
  that lies sick at home in the bed of honour.
RHODOPHIL
  Now let's have one common health, and so have done.
DORALICE
  Then for once I'll begin it. Here's to him that has the   115
  fairest lady of Sicily in masquerade tonight.
PALAMEDE
  This is such an obliging health, I'll kiss thee, dear rogue,
  for thy invention.
                          Kisses her

RHODOPHIL
  He who has this lady is a happy man, without dispute.
  (*aside*) I'm most concerned in this, I am sure.   120
PALAMEDE
  Was it not well found out, Rhodophil?
MELANTHA
  Ay, this was *bien trouvée* indeed.
DORALICE (*to* MELANTHA)
  I suppose I shall do you a kindness to enquire if you have
  not been in France, Sir?

108 *Old Chios* long-stored wine from the Greek island of Chios. In the seventeenth
    century wine was normally drunk very young, so this would be something special.
111 *seconds* second toast. The boy, Doralice, goes on to say to Palamede that he has no
    head for drink. The word 'second' occurs again shortly, at IV. iii. 158, meaning an
    assistant in a duel, and there may be a hint of that meaning here. The playful contest
    between Rhodophil and Palamede is also alarming and dangerous; Doralice is not
    prepared for it to come to a duel, as it finally almost does at V. i. 313. A duel between
    the two boys is a different matter, and quite clearly a game easily stopped at
    IV. iii. 158. But duelling, and the possibility of death, hovers excitingly behind the
    comedy, here as elsewhere. See I. i. 89–91.
112 *turtles* See note at III. i. 14. Rhodophil himself there uses the word of himself and
    his wife.
113 *of honour* honourable because chaste
121 *found out* thought of, devised; as in the French phrase that follows

MELANTHA
To do you service, Sir.   125

DORALICE (*saluting her*)
O, Monsieur, votre valet bien humble.

MELANTHA (*returning the salute*)
Votre esclave, Monsieur, de tout mon coeur.

DORALICE
I suppose, sweet Sir, you are the hope and joy of some
thriving citizen, who has pinched himself at home to breed
you abroad, where you have learnt your *exercices*, as it   130
appears most awkwardly, and are returned with the addition of a new-laced bosom and a clap to your good old
father, who looks at you with his mouth while you spout
French with your *man monsieur*.

PALAMEDE
Let me kiss thee again for that, dear rogue.   135

MELANTHA
And you, I imagine, are my young master whom your
mother durst not trust upon salt water, but left you to be
your own tutor at fourteen, to be very brisk and *entre-*
prenant, to endeavour to be debauched ere you have learnt
the knack on't, to value yourself upon a clap before you can   140
get it, and to make it the height of your ambition to get a
player for your mistress.

---

126 *O, Monsieur,* ed. (O, Monsieur, Q1)
127 *Votre* ed. (*Votrè* Q1)
130 *exercises* (Exercices Q1)

---

125 *To...Sir* an elaborate salute, in response to the elaborate tone of Doralice's
     question, with its elegant pleonastic negative
126 *O...humble* O, Sir, your most humble servant
127 *Votre...coeur* Your slave, Sir, with all my heart
132 *new-laced bosom* beribboned waistcoat in the French style
     a clap a dose of gonorrhoea
133 *with his mouth* his mouth as wide open as his eyes
134 *man monsieur* French servant. The California editors prefer to read 'Mon Monsieur'
     here with Q4, and they suggest that the boy 'addresses his father impudently with a
     "my good man" in French'; but the phrase 'Mon Monsieur', with no adjective bet-
     ween the two words, seems to me very dubious French, even for an English boy.
     The absence in Q1 of any comma after 'French' also supports the reading here,
     which would be a combination of English and French rather like '*good graces*' at
     II.i.44–5.
137 *upon salt water* to go abroad
138 *at fourteen* That is, after leaving school, at a point when other boys would be going
     to university.
138–9 *entreprenant* enterprising

RHODOPHIL (*embracing* MELANTHA)
    O dear young bully, thou hast tickled him with a *repartee*
    i'faith.

MELANTHA
    You are one of those that applaud our country plays, where   145
    drums, and trumpets, and blood, and wounds are wit.

RHODOPHIL
    Again, my boy? Let me kiss thee most abundantly.

DORALICE
    You are an admirer of the dull French poetry, which is so
    thin that it is the very leaf-gold of wit, the very wafers and
    whipped cream of sense, for which a man opens his mouth   150
    and gapes, to swallow nothing; and to be an admirer of
    such profound dulness, one must be endowed with a great
    perfection of impudence and ignorance.

PALAMEDE
    Let me embrace thee most vehemently.

MELANTHA (*advancing*)
    I'll sacrifice my life for French poetry.   155

DORALICE
    I'll die upon the spot for our country wit.

RHODOPHIL (*to* MELANTHA)
    Hold, hold, young Mars. Palamede, draw back your hero.

PALAMEDE
    'Tis time; I shall be drawn in for a second else, at the
    wrong weapon.

MELANTHA
    O that I were a man for thy sake!   160

DORALICE
    You'll be a man as soon as I shall.

Enter a MESSENGER *to* RHODOPHIL

---

146 *drums...wit* Dryden was usually on the side of drums. He defended himself in his
    essay *Of Heroique Playes*, which prefixed the printed version of *I The Conquest of
    Granada* in 1672, against 'those who object my frequent use of Drums and
    Trumpets'; and Buckingham in *The Rehearsal* depicts his playwright, Bayes (i.e.,
    Dryden), as quite carried away with such effects (IV. i. 18–22).

149–50 *wafers...cream* an elegant but insubstantial dessert, unlike the boiled puddings
    that established themselves as part of the native English cuisine in the seventeenth
    century

159 *wrong weapon* Palamede will find himself helping Doralice fight with a sword. But
    at the moment he is intent upon trying to 'second' a woman in a combat of another
    kind, with a sexual weapon.

161 *as...shall* That is, never.

MESSENGER
    Sir, the king has instant business with you.
    I saw the guard drawn up by your lieutenant
    Before the palace gate, ready to march.
RHODOPHIL
    'Tis somewhat sudden; say that I am coming.   165
                              Exit MESSENGER
    Now Palamede, what think you of this sport?
    This is some sudden tumult. Will you along?
PALAMEDE
    Yes, yes, I will go; but the devil take me if ever I was less
    in humour. Why the pox could they not have stayed their
    tumult till tomorrow? Then I had done my business, and   170
    been ready for them. Truth is, I had a little transitory
    crime to have committed first; and I am the worst man in
    the world at repenting, till a sin be thoroughly done. But
    what shall we do with the two boys?
RHODOPHIL
    Let them take a lodging in the house till the business be   175
    over.
DORALICE
    What, lie with a boy? For my part, I own it, I cannot
    endure to lie with a boy.
PALAMEDE
    The more's my sorrow I cannot accommodate you with a
    better bedfellow.   180
MELANTHA
    Let me die if I enter into a pair of sheets with him that
    hates the French.
DORALICE
    Pish, take no care for us, but leave us in the streets. I
    warrant you, as late as it is, I'll find my lodging as well as
    any drunken bully of them all.   185
RHODOPHIL (*aside*)
    I'll fight in mere revenge, and wreak my passion
    On all that spoil this hopeful assignation.
PALAMEDE
    I'm sure we fight in a good quarrel.
    Rogues may pretend religion, and the laws;
    But a kind mistress is the *good old cause*.   190
                                          Exeunt

166 *sport* That is, the sudden news, not the scene just past.
190 *good old cause* This was the description of the Puritan cause used by supporters,
    both in Cromwellian times and afterwards; here humorously applied instead to
    love intrigue. Puritans were strong in the City of London, and the bias of this play
    towards royalty and the court is clear. See note at Prologue 24.

Act IV, Scene iv

Enter PALMYRA, EUBULUS, HERMOGENES

PALMYRA
　You tell me wonders; that Leonidas
　Is Prince Theagenes, the late king's son.

EUBULUS
　It seemed as strange to him, as now to you,
　Before I had convinced him. But besides
　His great resemblance to the king his father,　　　　　5
　The queen his mother lives, secured by me
　In a religious house; to whom each year
　I brought the news of his increasing virtues.
　My last long absence from you both was caused
　By wounds which in my journey I received.　　　　　10
　When set upon by thieves, I lost those jewels
　And letters, which your dying mother left.

HERMOGENES
　The same he means, which since brought to the king,
　Made him first know he had a child alive.
　'Twas then my care of Prince Leonidas　　　　　15
　Caused me to say he was the usurper's son;
　Till after forced by your apparent danger,
　I made the true discovery of your birth,
　And once more hid my prince's.

Enter LEONIDAS

LEONIDAS
　Hermogenes and Eubulus, retire;　　　　　20
　Those of our party whom I left without
　Expect your aid and counsel.
　　　　　　　　　　　　　　　　Exeunt ambo

PALMYRA
　I should, Leonidas, congratulate
　This happy change of your exalted fate;
　But, as my joy, so you my wonder move.　　　　　25
　Your looks have more of business than of love,
　And your last words some great design did show.

LEONIDAS
　I frame not any to be hid from you.
　You in my love all my designs may see.

10 *received.* (receiv'd, Q1)
11 *thieves,* (thieves; Q1)

_____

22+ *ambo* together

But what have love and you designed for me?   30
Fortune once more has set the balance right:
First equalled us in lowness, then in height.
Both of us have so long, like gamesters, thrown,
Till fate comes round and gives to each his own.
As fate is equal, so may love appear: 35
Tell me at least what I must hope or fear.

PALMYRA
After so many proofs, how can you call
My love in doubt? Fear nothing, and hope all.
Think what a prince, with honour, may receive,
Or I may give without a parent's leave.   40

LEONIDAS
You give, and then restrain the grace you show;
As ostentatious priests, when souls they woo,
Promise their heaven to all, but grant to few.
But do for me what I have dared for you.
I did no argument from duty bring: 45
Duty's a name, and love's a real thing.

PALMYRA
Man's love may like wild torrents overflow;
Woman's as deep, but in its banks must go.
My love is mine; and that I can impart;
But cannot give my person with my heart.   50

LEONIDAS
Your love is then no gift.
For when the person it does not convey,
'Tis to give gold, and not to give the key.

PALMYRA
Then ask my father.

LEONIDAS   He detains my throne:
Who holds back mine, will hardly give his own.   55

PALMYRA
What then remains?

LEONIDAS   That I must have recourse
To arms; and take my love and crown by force.
Hermogenes is forming the design,
And with him all the brave and loyal join.

PALMYRA
And is it thus you court Palmyra's bed?   60
Can she the murderer of her parent wed?
Desist from force: so much you well may give
To love and me, to let my father live.

LEONIDAS
Each act of mine my love to you has shown;

But you, who tax my want of it, have none.   65
You bid me part with you and let him live;
But they should nothing ask who nothing give.

PALMYRA

I give what virtue and what duty can,
In vowing ne'er to wed another man.

LEONIDAS

You will be forced to be Argaleon's wife.   70

PALMYRA

I'll keep my promise, though I lose my life.

LEONIDAS

Then you lose love, for which we both contend;
For life is but the means, but love's the end.

PALMYRA

Our souls shall love hereafter.

LEONIDAS   I much fear,
That soul which could deny the body here   75
To taste of love, would be a niggard there.

PALMYRA

Then 'tis past hope: our cruel fate, I see,
Will make a sad divorce 'twixt you and me.
For if you force employ, by heaven I swear,
And all blessed beings, –

LEONIDAS   Your rash oath forbear.   80

PALMYRA

I never –

LEONIDAS   Hold once more. But yet, as he
Who 'scapes a dangerous leap, looks back to see,
So I desire, now I am past my fear,
To know what was that oath you meant to swear.

PALMYRA

I meant that if you hazarded your life,   85
Or sought my father's, ne'er to be your wife.

LEONIDAS

See now, Palmyra, how unkind you prove!
Could you with so much ease forswear my love?

PALMYRA

You force me with your ruinous design.

LEONIDAS

Your father's life is more your care than mine.   90

PALMYRA

You wrong me, 'tis not; though it ought to be;
You are my care, heaven knows, as well as he.

LEONIDAS

If now the execution I delay,

My honour and my subjects I betray.
All is prepared for the just enterprise,   95
And the whole city will tomorrow rise.
The leaders of the party are within,
And Eubulus has sworn that he will bring,
To head their arms, the person of their king.

PALMYRA
In telling this, you make me guilty too;   100
I therefore must discover what I know.
What honour bids you do, nature bids me prevent;
But kill me first, and then pursue your black intent.

LEONIDAS
Palmyra, no; you shall not need to die;
Yet I'll not trust so strict a piety.   105
[*calls out*] Within there.

Enter EUBULUS

                    Eubulus, a guard prepare;
Here, I commit this prisoner to your care.

Kisses PALMYRA'*s hand; then gives it to* EUBULUS

PALMYRA
Leonidas, I never thought these bands
Could e'er be given me by a lover's hands.

LEONIDAS (*kneeling*)
Palmyra, thus your judge himself arraigns.   110
He who imposed these bonds still wears your chains.
When you to love or duty false must be,
Or to your father guilty, or to me,
These chains alone remain to set you free.

Noise of swords clashing

POLYDAMAS (*within*)
Secure these first; then search the inner room.   115

LEONIDAS
From whence do these tumultuous clamours come?

Enter HERMOGENES *hastily*

HERMOGENES
We are betrayed; and there remains alone
This comfort, that your person is not known.

Enter [POLYDAMAS] *the king,* ARGALEON, RHODOPHIL,
     PALAMEDE, *guards; some like citizens as prisoners*

101 *discover* reveal

POLYDAMAS
  What mean these midnight consultations here,
  Where I like an unsummoned guest appear?   120
LEONIDAS
  Sir –
ARGALEON There needs no excuse; 'tis understood;
  You were all watching for your prince's good.
POLYDAMAS
  My reverend city friends, you are well met!
  On what great work were your grave wisdoms set?
  Which of my actions were you scanning here?   125
  What French invasion have you found to fear?
LEONIDAS
  They are my friends; and come, Sir, with intent
  To take their leaves before my banishment.
POLYDAMAS (*seeing* PALMYRA)
  Your exile in both sexes friends can find:
  I see the ladies, like the men, are kind.   130
PALMYRA (*kneeling*)
  Alas, I came but –
POLYDAMAS   Add not to your crime
  A lie: I'll hear you speak some other time.
  How? Eubulus! Nor time, nor thy disguise,
  Can keep thee undiscovered from my eyes.
  A guard there; seize them all.   135
RHODOPHIL
  Yield, Sir. What use of valour can be shown?
PALAMEDE
  One, and unarmed, against a multitude!
LEONIDAS
  O for a sword!

He reaches at one of the guards' halberds, and is seized behind

          I would not lose my breath
  In fruitless prayers; but beg a speedy death.
PALMYRA
  O spare Leonidas, and punish me.   140

---

119 *these* F (this Q1)
138 *LEONIDAS* O F (O Q1)

123–6 *My...fear* The City of London was a centre of Puritan opposition at this time to
  any alliance with the Catholic French against the Dutch, who were both Protestants
  and merchants. The French and Catholic sympathies of this play, by contrast, are
  clear; the Prologue begins with an approving reference to the coming Dutch war.

POLYDAMAS
    Mean girl, thou wantst an advocate for thee.
    Now the mysterious knot will be untied:
    Whether the young king lives, or where he died.
    Tomorrow's dawn shall the dark riddle clear,
    Crown all my joys, and dissipate my fear.   145

                                        Exeunt omnes

Act V, Scene i

PALAMEDE, STRATON; PALAMEDE *with a letter in his hand*

PALAMEDE
    This evening, sayst thou? Will they both be here?
STRATON
    Yes, Sir; both my old master, and your mistress's father.
    The old gentlemen ride hard this journey. They say it shall
    be the last time they will see the town; and both of them are
    so pleased with this marriage which they have concluded   5
    for you, that I am afraid they will live some years longer to
    trouble you, with the joy of it.
PALAMEDE
    But this is such an unreasonable thing, to impose upon me
    to be married tomorrow. 'Tis hurrying a man to execution
    without giving him time to say his prayers.   10
STRATON
    Yet, if I might advise you, Sir, you should not delay it; for
    your younger brother comes up with them, and is got already
    into their favours. He has gained much upon my old master
    by finding fault with innkeepers' bills, and by starving us
    and our horses to show his frugality; and he is very well   15
    with your mistress's father, by giving him receipts for the
    spleen, gout, and scurvy, and other infirmities of old age.
PALAMEDE
    I'll rout him, and his country education. Pox on him, I
    remember him before I travelled; he had nothing in him
    but mere jockey; used to talk loud, and make matches, and   20

---

141 *Mean* wretched
    thou...thee That is, you need someone to plead for you; you should not yourself be
    pleading for another.
16 *receipts* remedies
20 *jockey* That is, he was a 'little Jack', a mere country boy, obsessed with country
    sports.
    make matches back himself against others, probably in horse races

was all for the crack of the field. Sense and wit were as
much banished from his discourse, as they are when the
court goes out of town to a horse race. Go now and provide
your master's lodgings.

STRATON

I go, Sir.   25

Exit

PALAMEDE

It vexes me to the heart, to leave all my designs with Doralice
unfinished. To have flown her so often to a mark, and still to
be bobbed at retrieve. If I had but once enjoyed her, though
I could not have satisfied my stomach with the feast, at
least I should have relished my mouth a little; but now –   30

Enter PHILOTIS

PHILOTIS

Oh, Sir, you are happily met. I was coming to find you.

PALAMEDE

From your lady, I hope.

PHILOTIS

Partly from her, but more especially from myself. She has
just now received a letter from her father, with an absolute
command to dispose herself to marry you tomorrow.   35

PALAMEDE

And she takes it to the death?

PHILOTIS

Quite contrary. The letter could never have come in a more
lucky minute, for it found her in an ill humour with a rival
of yours, that shall be nameless, about the pronunciation of
a French word.   40

PALAMEDE

Count Rhodophil; never disguise it, I know the *amour*. But
I hope you took the occasion to strike in for me?

---

34 *father* Q2 (Fathet Q1)

---

21 *crack of the field* the favourite horse in the race meeting, the one most boasted about
23 *court...race* Charles II was passionately devoted to horse racing, and often went to
   Newmarket for the races.
27 *mark* quarry. Doralice is here the hawk flown by Palamede, and his own body is the
   quarry.
28 *bobbed* cheated
   retrieve the second or subsequent flight of a target bird once already sprung.
   Palamede has failed not only in his first attempt but subsequently, 'at retrieve', to
   enable Doralice to reach her target. Note Palamede's sudden burst of imagery from
   country sports, the influence of his little brother upon him.

PHILOTIS
It was my good fortune to do you some small service in it.
For your sake I discommended him all over: clothes,
person, humour, behaviour, everything; and to sum up all,   45
told her, it was impossible to find a married man that was
otherwise; for they were all so mortified at home with their
wives' ill humours, that they could never recover themselves to be company abroad.

PALAMEDE
Most divinely urged!   50

PHILOTIS
Then I took occasion to commend your good qualities: as,
the sweetness of your humour, the comeliness of your
person, your good mien, your valour; but above all your
liberality.

PALAMEDE
I vow to God I had like to have forgot that good quality in   55
myself, if thou hadst not remembered me on't. Here are
five pieces for thee.

PHILOTIS
Lord, you have the softest hand, Sir! It would do a woman
good to touch it. Count Rhodophil's is not half so soft;
for I remember I felt it once, when he gave me ten pieces   60
for my new year's gift.

PALAMEDE
O, I understand you, Madam; you shall find my hand as
soft again as Count Rhodophil's. There are twenty pieces
for you. The former was but a retaining fee; now I hope
you'll plead for me.   65

PHILOTIS
Your own merits speak enough. Be sure only to ply her
with French words, and I'll warrant you'll do your business.
Here are a list of her phrases for this day: use them to her
upon all occasions, and foil her at her own weapon; for she's
like one of the old Amazons, she'll never marry except it be   70
the man who has first conquered her.

---

53 *mien* bearing, air
57 *pieces* These are either gold guineas or twenty shilling silver pieces. Gregory King
   in the late seventeenth century reckoned a subsistence allowance at between £7 and
   £8 per head per annum, and Pepys in 1662 thought the £7 per month he spent on
   housekeeping was excessive; so this is a substantial tip.
62–3 *as soft again* twice as soft

PALAMEDE
I'll be sure to follow your advice. But you'll forget to
further my design.

PHILOTIS
What, do you think I'll be ungrateful? – But, however, if
you distrust my memory, put some token on my finger to   75
remember it by: that diamond there would do admirably.

PALAMEDE
There 'tis; and I ask your pardon heartily for calling your
memory into question. I assure you I'll trust it another
time, without putting you to the trouble of another token.

Enter PALMYRA *and* ARTEMIS

ARTEMIS
Madam, this way the prisoners are to pass;   80
Here you may see Leonidas.

PALMYRA
Then here I'll stay, and follow him to death.

Enter MELANTHA *hastily*

MELANTHA
O, here's her highness! Now is my time to introduce myself,
and to make my court to her, in my new French phrases.
Stay, let me read my catalogue – *suite, figure, chagrin,*   85
naiveté, and let me die for the parenthesis of all.

PALAMEDE (*aside*)
Do, persecute her; and I'll persecute thee as fast in thy
own dialect.

MELANTHA
Madam the Princess! Let me die but this is a most horrid
spectacle, to see a person who makes so grand a *figure* in the 90
court without the *suite* of a princess, and entertaining your
chagrin all alone. [*aside*] *Naiveté* should have been there,
but the disobedient word would not come in.

PALMYRA [*to* ARTEMIS]
What is she, Artemis?

ARTEMIS [*to* PALMYRA]
An impertinent lady, Madam, very ambitious of being   95
known to your Highness.

PALAMEDE (*to* MELANTHA)
Let me die, Madam, if I have not waited you here these two

90 *figure* ed. (figure Q1)

---

86 *for…all* bracketing all the others. 'Let me die' is Melantha's most often repeated
phrase.

long hours, without so much as the *suite* of a single servant
to attend me; entertaining myself with my own *chagrin*,
till I had the honour to see your Ladyship, who are a person   100
that makes so considerable a *figure* in the court.

MELANTHA

Truce with your *douceurs*, good servant; you see I am
addressing to the princess; pray do not *embarrass* me –
embarrass me! What a delicious French word do you make
me lose upon you too! (*to the princess*) Your Highness,   105
Madam, will please to *pardon* the *bévue* which I made, in not
sooner finding you out to be a princess; but let me die if
this *éclaircissement* which is made this day of your quality
does not ravish me; and give me leave to tell you –

PALAMEDE

But first give me leave to tell you, Madam, that I have so   110
great a *tender* for your person, and such a *penchant* to do
you service, that –

MELANTHA

What, must I still be troubled with your *sottises?* (There's
another word lost that I meant for the princess, with a
mischief to you.) But your Highness, Madam –   115

PALAMEDE

But your Ladyship, Madam –

Enter LEONIDAS *guarded, and led over the stage*

MELANTHA

Out upon him, how he looks, Madam! Now he's found no
prince, he is the strangest *figure* of a man. How could I
make that *coup d'étourdi* to think him one?

PALMYRA

Away, impertinent – My dear Leonidas!   120

LEONIDAS

My dear Palmyra!

PALMYRA

Death shall never part us;
My destiny is yours.

He is led off; she follows

101 *figure* ed. (figure Q1)
106 *pardon* (pardon Q1)
111 *tender* (tender Q1)
115 *you.* Q3 (you Q1)
118 *figure* ed. (figure Q1)

102 *douceurs* pretty sentiments
114–15 *with…you* plague upon you

MELANTHA
  Impertinent! Oh I am the most unfortunate person this day
  breathing: that the princess should thus *rompre en visière*,   125
  without occasion. Let me die but I'll follow her to death,
  till I make my peace.
PALAMEDE (*holding her*)
  And let me die but I'll follow you to the infernals till you
  pity me.
MELANTHA (*turning towards him angrily*)
  Ay, 'tis long of you that this *malheur* is fallen upon me.   130
  Your impertinence has put me out of the good graces of the
  princess, and all that, which has ruined me and all that,
  and therefore let me die but I'll be revenged, and all that.
PALAMEDE
  Façon, façon, you must and shall love me, and all that; for
  my old man is coming up, and all that; and I am *désespéré*   135
  au dernier, and will not be disinherited, and all that.
MELANTHA
  How durst you interrupt me so *mal à propos,* when you
  knew I was addressing to the princess?
PALAMEDE
  But why would you address yourself so much *à contretemps*
  then?   140
MELANTHA
  Ah *mal peste!*
PALAMEDE
  Ah *j'enrage!*

---

142 *j* ed.(*I* Q1)

---

125 *rompre en visière* fall out with me
128 *infernals* infernal regions
130 *long of* because of
    malheur misfortune
134 *Façon, façon* The French phrase 'point de façon' in a certain context means 'get on
    and do the thing without fussy delay'; here Palamede seems to be saying 'this is all
    beside the point, beside the point; what you must do is love me'.
135–6 *désespéré au dernier* desperate to the last degree
137 *mal à propos* impertinently. Palmyra has just dismissed Melantha with the same
    charge in English.
139 *à contretemps* at the wrong time
141 *mal peste* beastly nuisance
142 *j'enrage* I'm losing my temper

PHILOTIS
> *Radoucissez-vous, de grâce, Madame; vous êtes bien en colère*
> *pour peu de chose. Vous n'entendez pas la raillerie galante.*

MELANTHE (*cries*)
> A d'autres, à d'autres. He mocks himself of me, he abuses   145
> me: ah me unfortunate!

PHILOTIS
> You mistake him, Madam, he does but accommodate his
> phrase to your refined language. *Ah, qu'il est un cavalier*
> *accompli!* (*to him*) Pursue your point, Sir –

PALAMEDE (*singing*)
> > *Ah qu'il fait beau dans ces bocages;*   150
> > *Ah que le ciel donne un beau jour!*
> There I was with you, with a *menuet.*

MELANTHA (*laughs*)
> Let me die now but this singing is fine, and extremely French
> in him. (*crying*) But then, that he should use my own
> words, as it were in contempt of me, I cannot bear it.   155

PALAMEDE (*singing*)
> > *Ces beaux séjours, ces doux ramages –*

MELANTHA (*singing after him*)
> > *Ces beaux séjours, ces doux ramages,*
> > *Ces beaux séjours, nous invitent à l'amour!*
> (*laughing*) Let me die but he sings *en cavalier*, and so
> humours the cadence.   160

---

145 *A d'autres, à d'autres* ed. (*Ad' autres, ad' autres* Q1)

143–4 *Radoucissez-vous...galante* Calm yourself, I beg you, Madam; you are angry
  about a trifle. This is simply courtly wit.
145 *He...of me* a literal translation of the French 'il se moque de' into frenchified
  English
     abuses The word is good plain English for 'uses me ill', but no doubt Melantha has
     the French verb in mind as well, especially since her English has suddenly become
     even more frenchified than usual.
146 *me unfortunate* Frenchified English again
148–9 *qu'il...accompli* how accomplished a gentleman he is!
150–1 *Ah...jour* O how pleasant it is in these groves; / O what a fine day the heavens
  give us! This song (to line 158) and the one following (lines 161–2) are from the end
  of Molière's *Le Bourgeois Gentilhomme* (1670).
157–8 *Ces...l'amour* These pleasant spots, these sweet leafy arbours, / These pleasant
  spots invite us to love!
159 *en cavalier* as a gentleman should

PALAMEDE (*singing again*)
> *Vois, ma Clymène, vois sous ce chêne*
> *S'entrebaiser ces oiseaux amoureux!*

Let me die now but that was fine. Ah, now, for three or
four brisk Frenchmen to be put into masquing habits, and
to sing it on a theatre, how witty it would be! And then to   165
dance helter skelter to a *chanson à boire: toute la terre, toute
la terre est à moi!* What's matter though it were made and
sung two or three years ago in *cabarets*, how it would attract
the admiration especially of everyone that's an *éveillé!*

MELANTHA (PALAMEDE *sings while she speaks*)
> Well, I begin to have a *tender* for you; but yet, upon con-   170
> dition that – when we are married, you –

PHILOTIS [*to* PALAMEDE]
> You must drown her voice. If she makes her French
> conditions, you are a slave for ever.

MELANTHA
> First, will you engage – that –

PALAMEDE (*louder*)
> Fa, la, la, la, &c.   175

MELANTHA
> Will you hear the conditions?

PALAMEDE
> No, I will hear no conditions! I am resolved to win you *en
> français*, to be very airy, with abundance of noise, and no
> sense. Fa, la, la, la, &c.

MELANTHA
> Hold, hold. I am vanquished with your *gaîté d'esprit.* I am   180
> yours, and will be yours, *sans nulle réserve, ni condition;* and
> let me die if I do not think myself the happiest nymph in
> Sicily – My dear French dear, stay but a *minute*, till I

170 *tender* (tender Q1)
174 – *that* – (– that Q1)
183 *minute* (minuite Q1)

161–2 *Vois...amoureux* See, my Clymène, see under this oak, / How these amorous
    birds exchange kisses!
165 *on a theatre* on a stage; as in Molière's play
166 *chanson à boire* drinking song
166–7 *toute...moi* all the earth is mine!
168 *cabarets* taverns
169 *éveillé* man alert to fashion and wit
180 *gaîté d'esprit* gaiety of spirit
181 *sans...condition* unreservedly and unconditionally

raccommode myself with the princess; and then I am yours
jusqu'à la mort. [*to* PHILOTIS] *Allons donc.*   185

              Exeunt MELANTHA, PHILOTIS

PALAMEDE (*solus, fanning himself with his hat*)

I never thought before that wooing was so laborious an
exercise. If she were worth a million, I have deserved her.
And now, methinks, too, with taking all this pains for her,
I begin to like her. 'Tis so; I have known many, who never
cared for hare nor partridge, but those they caught them-   190
selves would eat heartily. The pains, and the story a man
tells of the taking of them, makes the meat go down more
pleasantly. Besides, last night I had a sweet dream of her
and, God, she I have once dreamed of, I am stark mad till I
enjoy her, let her be never so ugly.   195

              Enter DORALICE

DORALICE

Who's that you are so mad to enjoy, Palamede?

PALAMEDE

You may easily imagine that, sweet Doralice.

DORALICE

More easily than you think I can. I met just now with a
certain man, who came to you with letters from a certain
old gentleman yclept your father; whereby I am given to   200
understand that tomorrow you are to take an oath in the
church to be grave henceforward, to go ill-dressed and
slovenly, to get heirs for your estate, and to dandle them
for your diversion; and in short that love and courtship are
to be no more.   205

PALAMEDE

Now have I so much shame to be thus apprehended in the
manner, that I can neither speak nor look upon you. I have
abundance of grace in me, that I find. But if you have any
spark of true friendship in you, retire a little with me to
the next room that has a couch or bed in it, and bestow your 210

---

184 *raccommode* reconcile
185 *jusqu'à la mort* till death
    Allons donc come then
186 sp *solus* alone
200 *yclept* called; an archaic word jokily used
206–7 *in the manner* in the business (of getting married)
208–11 *grace; friendship; charity; comfort* These four words occurring in this passage
    must all be taken to have sexual connotation.
210 *next* nearest. See Prologue 35.

charity upon a poor dying man. A little comfort from a
mistress, before a man is going to give himself in marriage,
is as good as a lusty dose of strong water to a dying male-
factor; it takes away the sense of hell and hanging from him.

DORALICE
No, good Palamede, I must not be so injurious to your   215
bride. 'Tis ill drawing from the bank today when all your
ready money is payable tomorrow.

PALAMEDE
A wife is only to have the ripe fruit that falls of itself; but
a wise man will always preserve a shaking for a mistress.

DORALICE
But a wife for the first quarter is a mistress.   220

PALAMEDE
But when the second comes.

DORALICE
When it does come, you are so given to variety, that you
would make a wife of me in another quarter.

PALAMEDE
No never, except I were married to you. Married people
can never oblige one another, for all they do is duty, and   225
consequently there can be no thanks. But love is more
frank and generous than he is honest; he's a liberal giver,
but a cursed paymaster.

DORALICE
I declare I will have no gallant; but if I would, he should
never be a married man. A married man is but a mistress's   230
half-servant, as a clergyman is but the king's half-subject.
For a man to come to me that smells of the wife! 'Slife, I
would as soon wear her old gown after her as her husband.

PALAMEDE
Yet 'tis a kind of fashion to wear a princess's cast shoes; you
see the country ladies buy them to be fine in them.   235

DORALICE
Yes, a princess's shoes may be worn after her because they
keep their fashion by being so very little used; but generally
a married man is the creature of the world the most out of

213 *strong water* spirits. Those about to be hanged were usually offered alcohol.

216–17 *drawing...payable* The image of spending money is often associated, as here,
  with ejaculation.

222–3 *you would...quarter* In another three months you would reduce me, too, to the
  status of a wife by taking a fresh mistress.

227–8 *he's...paymaster* Love *gives* freely, but only grudgingly pays what is demanded
  as due.

229 *gallant* the male equivalent of a mistress

fashion. His behaviour is dumpish, his discourse his wife
and family, his habit so much neglected it looks as if that   240
were married too: his hat is married, his peruke is married,
his breeches are married, and if we could look within his
breeches, we should find him married there too.

PALAMEDE
Am I then to be discarded for ever? Pray do but mark how
terrible that word sounds. For ever! It has a very damned   245
sound, Doralice.

DORALICE
Ay, for ever! It sounds as hellishly to me as it can do to you,
but there's no help for it.

PALAMEDE
Yet if we had but once enjoyed one another; but then once
only is worse than not at all; it leaves a man with such a   250
lingering after it.

DORALICE
For aught I know 'tis better that we have not; we might upon
trial have liked each other less, as many a man and woman
that have loved as desperately as we, and yet when they
came to possession, have sighed and cried to themselves: is   255
this all?

PALAMEDE
That is only if the servant were not found a man of this
world; but if upon trial we had not liked each other, we had
certainly left loving; and faith, that's the greater happiness
of the two.   260

DORALICE
'Tis better as 'tis; we have drawn off already as much of
our love as would run clear. After possessing, the rest is
but jealousies, and disquiets, and quarrelling, and piecing.

PALAMEDE
Nay, after one great quarrel there's never any sound
piecing; the love is apt to break in the same place again.   265

DORALICE
I declare I would never renew a love. That's like him who
trims an old coach for ten years together; he might buy a
new one better cheap.

---

239 *dumpish* dull, spiritless
257–8 *man of this world* proper man
262 *run clear* The image is of drawing wine or beer from a cask for as long as the liquid is
    clear, before it is clouded by sediment.
263 *piecing* piecing together, making up a quarrel. There is a pun perhaps with 'peace'.
268 *better cheap* as a better bargain

PALAMEDE

Well, Madam, I am convinced that 'tis best for us not to
have enjoyed; but God, the strongest reason is, because I   270
cannot help it.

DORALICE

The only way to keep us new to one another is never to
enjoy, as they keep grapes by hanging them upon a line:
they must touch nothing if you would preserve them fresh.

PALAMEDE

But then they wither and grow dry in the very keeping.   275
However I shall have a warmth for you, and an eagerness
every time I see you; and if I chance to outlive Melantha –

DORALICE

And if I chance to outlive Rhodophil –

PALAMEDE

Well, I'll cherish my body as much as I can upon that hope.
'Tis true I would not directly murder the wife of my bosom; 280
but to kill her civilly, by the way of kindness, I'll put as
fair as another man. I'll begin tomorrow night, and be very
wrathful with her, that's resolved on.

DORALICE

Well, Palamede, here's my hand; I'll venture to be your
second wife, for all your threatenings.   285

PALAMEDE

In the mean time I'll watch you hourly, as I would the
ripeness of a melon, and I hope you'll give me leave now
and then to look on you, and to see if you are not ready to be
cut yet.

DORALICE

No, no, that must not be, Palamede, for fear the gardener   290
should come and catch you taking up the glass.

Enter RHODOPHIL

RHODOPHIL (*aside*)

Billing so sweetly! Now I am confirmed in my suspicions.
I must put an end to this, ere it go further. (*to* DORALICE)
Cry you mercy, spouse, I fear I have interrupted your
recreations.   295

DORALICE

What recreations?

---

281 *by the way of kindness* in a humane way
281–2 *put as fair* think as legitimate
291 *glass* as in a cold frame. The sexual connotation is clear.
292 *Billing* kissing. Like a pair of birds, like turtles in fact. See III. i. 14 and IV. iii. 112.

RHODOPHIL
Nay no excuses, good spouse; I saw fair hand conveyed to
lip, and pressed, as though you had been squeezing soft
wax together for an indenture. Palamede, you and I must
clear this reckoning. Why would you have seduced my wife?   300
PALAMEDE
Why would you have debauched my mistress?
RHODOPHIL
What do you think of that civil couple that played at a game
called hide and seek last evening in the grotto?
PALAMEDE
What do you think of that innocent pair who made it their
pretence to seek for others, but came indeed to hide them-   305
selves there?
RHODOPHIL
All things considered, I begin vehemently to suspect that
the young gentleman I found in your company last night
was a certain youth of my acquaintance.
PALAMEDE
And I have an odd imagination, that you could never have   310
suspected my small gallant if your little villainous
Frenchman had not been a false brother.
RHODOPHIL
Farther arguments are needless. Draw off. I shall speak to
you now by the way of Bilbo.

Claps his hand to his sword

PALAMEDE
And I shall answer you by the way of Dangerfield.   315

Claps his hand on his

DORALICE
Hold, hold. Are not you two a couple of mad fighting fools
to cut one another's throats for nothing?
PALAMEDE
How for nothing? He courts the woman I must marry.
RHODOPHIL
And he courts you whom I have married.
DORALICE
But you can neither of you be jealous of what you love not.   320

---

299 *indenture* sealed agreement
314 *Bilbo* a sword; originally a sword from Bilbao in Spain
315 *Dangerfield* It is difficult to make satisfactory sense of this reference; perhaps there
was a contemporary London swordsmith called Dangerfield.

RHODOPHIL
Faith I am jealous, and that makes me partly suspect that I love you better than I thought.

DORALICE
Pish! A mere jealousy of honour.

RHODOPHIL
God, I am afraid there's something else in it; for Palamede has wit, and if he loves you there's something more in ye 325
than I have found. Some rich mine, for aught I know, that I have not yet discovered.

PALAMEDE
'Slife, what's this? Here's an argument for me to love Melantha; for he has loved her, and he has wit too, and for aught I know there may be a mine. But if there be, I am 330
resolved I'll dig for it.

DORALICE (*to* RHODOPHIL)
Then I have found my account in raising your jealousy. O 'tis the most delicate sharp sauce to a cloyed stomach! It will give you a new edge, Rhodophil.

RHODOPHIL
And a new point too, Doralice, if I could be sure thou art 335
honest.

DORALICE
If you are wise, believe me for your own sake. Love and religion have but one thing to trust to, that's a good sound faith. Consider, if I have played false, you can never find it out by any experiment you can make upon me. 340

RHODOPHIL
No? Why, suppose I had a delicate screwed gun: if I left her clean and found her foul, I should discover, to my cost, she had been shot in.

DORALICE
But if you left her clean, and found her only rusty, you would discover, to your shame, she was only so for want of 345
shooting.

PALAMEDE
Rhodophil, you know me too well to imagine I speak for fear; and therefore, in consideration of our past friendship, I will tell you, and bind it by all things holy, that Doralice is innocent. 350

---

332 *account* reckoning, worth
341 *delicate screwed gun* finely rifled gun. The copulatory imagery is clear.
346 *shooting* an easy image for ejaculation

RHODOPHIL
   Friend, I will believe you, and vow the same for your
Melantha. But the devil on't is, how shall we keep them so?

PALAMEDE
   What dost think of a blessed community betwixt us four, for
the solace of the women and relief of the men? Methinks it
would be a pleasant kind of life: wife and husband for the   355
standing dish, and mistress and gallant for the dessert.

RHODOPHIL
   But suppose the wife and the mistress should both long for
the standing dish. How should they be satisfied together?

PALAMEDE
   In such a case they must draw lots. And yet that would not do
neither, for they would both be wishing for the longest cut.   360

RHODOPHIL
   Then I think, Palamede, we had as good make a firm
league not to invade each other's propriety.

PALAMEDE
   Content, say I. From henceforth let all acts of hostility
cease betwixt us; and that in the usual form of treaties, as
well by sea as by land, and in all fresh waters.   365

DORALICE
   I will add but one proviso: that whoever breaks the league,
either by war abroad, or by neglect at home, both the women
shall revenge themselves by the help of the other party.

RHODOPHIL
   That's but reasonable. Come away, Doralice; I have a great
temptation to be sealing articles in private.   370

PALAMEDE (*claps him on the shoulder*)
   Hast thou so?
   Fall on, Macduff,
   And cursed be he that first cries: hold, enough.

   Enter POLYDAMAS, PALMYRA, ARTEMIS, ARGALEON; *after*
     them EUBULUS *and* HERMOGENES, *guarded*

352 *so?* Q2 (so. Q1)
360 *cut.* F (out? Q1)

---

356 *standing dish* fixed main dish (as distinct from the varied dessert). 'Standing' must
   insinuate erection here, and perhaps 'dessert' signifies something more trifling than
   copulation.
360 *longest cut* longest straw, with a glance perhaps at the size of erection.
362 *propriety* The play ends as it began. See I. i. 75.
370 *sealing articles* sealing the treaty, consummating the agreement
372 *Fall on* Macbeth's words, from the end of Shakespeare's play, are in fact: 'Lay on,
   Macduff, / And damn'd be him that first cries hold, enough.'

PALMYRA
Sir, on my knees I beg you.
POLYDAMAS
Away, I'll hear no more.   375
PALMYRA
For my dead mother's sake; you say you loved her,
And tell me I resemble her. Thus she
Had begged.
POLYDAMAS   And thus had I denied her.
PALMYRA
You must be merciful.
ARGALEON [to the king]   You must be constant.
POLYDAMAS
Go, bear them to the torture; you have boasted   380
You have a king to head you. I would know
To whom I must resign.
EUBULUS   This is our recompense
For serving thy dead queen.
HERMOGENES   And education
Of thy daughter.
ARGALEON
You are too modest, in not naming all   385
His obligations to you. Why did you
Omit his son, the Prince Leonidas?
POLYDAMAS
That imposture
I had forgot; their tortures shall be doubled.
HERMOGENES
You please me; I shall die the sooner.   390
EUBULUS
No; could I live an age, and still be racked,
I still would keep the secret.

As they are going off, enter LEONIDAS, *guarded*

LEONIDAS
Oh whither do you hurry innocence!
If you have any justice, spare their lives;
Or if I cannot make you just, at least   395
I'll teach you to more purpose to be cruel.
PALMYRA
Alas, what does he seek!
LEONIDAS
Make me the object of your hate and vengeance!
Are these decrepit bodies, worn to ruin,
Just ready of themselves to fall asunder   400

And to let drop the soul,
Are these fit subjects for a rack and tortures?
Where would you fasten any hold upon them?
Place pains on me; united fix them here;
I have both youth and strength and soul to bear them.　　405
And if they merit death, then I much more,
Since 'tis for me they suffer.
HERMOGENES　　　　　　　　　　　Heaven forbid
We should redeem our pains or worthless lives
By our exposing yours.
EUBULUS
Away with us. Farewell, Sir.　　　　　　　　　　410
I only suffer in my fears for you.
ARGALEON (*aside*)
So much concerned for him? Then my
Suspicion's true.

Whispers [to] the king

PALMYRA
Hear yet my last request, for poor Leonidas;
Or take my life with his.　　　　　　　　　　　415
ARGALEON (*to the king*)
Rest satisfied; Leonidas is he.
POLYDAMAS [*to* ARGALEON]
I am amazed. What must be done?
ARGALEON [*to the king*]
Command his execution instantly.
Give him not leisure to discover it;
He may corrupt the soldiers.　　　　　　　　　　420
POLYDAMAS
Hence with that traitor; bear him to his death.
Haste there, and see my will performed.
LEONIDAS
Nay, then I'll die like him the gods have made me.
Hold, gentlemen; I am –

ARGALEON stops his mouth

ARGALEON
Thou art a traitor; 'tis not fit to hear thee.　　　425
LEONIDAS (*getting loose a little*)
I say I am the –
ARGALEON (*again stopping his mouth*)
So; gag him and lead him off.
　　　　　　　LEONIDAS, HERMOGENES, EUBULUS *led off;*
　　　　　　　POLYDAMAS *and* ARGALEON *follow*

PALMYRA [aside]
   Duty and love by turns possess my soul,
   And struggle for a fatal victory.
   I will discover he's the king. Ah no.   430
   That will perhaps save him,
   But then I am guilty of a father's ruin.
   What shall I do, or not do? Either way
   I must destroy a parent, or a lover.
   Break heart; for that's the least of ills to me,   435
   And death the only cure. (swoons)

ARTEMIS
   Help, help the princess.

RHODOPHIL
   Bear her gently hence, where she may
   Have more succour.

     She is borne off: ARTEMIS *follows her; shouts within, and*
                  clashing of swords

PALAMEDE
   What noise is that?   440

         Enter AMALTHEA *running*

AMALTHEA
   Oh, gentlemen, if you have loyalty
   Or courage, show it now. Leonidas
   Broke on the sudden from his guards, and snatching
   A sword from one, his back against the scaffold,
   Bravely defends himself; and owns aloud   445
   He is our long lost king, found for this moment,
   But if your valours help not, lost for ever.
   Two of his guards, moved by the sense of virtue,
   Are turned for him, and there they stand at bay
   Against an host of foes.

RHODOPHIL   Madam, no more.   450
   We lose time: my command or my example
   May move the soldiers to the better cause.
   (to PALAMEDE) You'll second me?

PALAMEDE
   Or die with you. No subject e'er can meet
   A nobler fate than at his sovereign's feet.   455

                      Exeunt

Clashing of swords within and shouts; enter LEONIDAS,
RHODOPHIL, PALAMEDE, EUBULUS, HERMOGENES *and their
party, victorious;* POLYDAMAS *and* ARGALEON, *disarmed*

LEONIDAS
    That I survive the dangers of this day,
    Next to the gods, brave friends, be yours the honour.
    And let heaven witness for me, that my joy
    Is not more great for this my right restored,
    Than 'tis, that I have power to recompense   460
    Your loyalty and valour. Let mean princes,
    Of abject souls, fear to reward great actions;
    I mean to show,
    That whatsoe'er subjects like you dare merit,
    A king like me dares give –   465
RHODOPHIL
    You make us blush we have deserved so little.
PALAMEDE
    And yet instruct us how to merit more.
LEONIDAS
    And as I would be just in my rewards,
    So should I in my punishments. These two,
    This the usurper of my crown, the other   470
    Of my Palmyra's love, deserve that death
    Which both designed for me.
POLYDAMAS   And we expect it.
ARGALEON
    I have too long been happy to live wretched.
POLYDAMAS
    And I too long have governed, to desire
    A life without an empire.   475
LEONIDAS
    You are Palmyra's father; and as such,
    Though not a king, shall have obedience paid
    From him who is one. Father, in that name
    All injuries forgot and duty owned.

Embraces him

POLYDAMAS
    O, had I known you could have been this king,   480

455+ *enter…disarmed* The ease and convenience with which the entire reversal of
fortune occurs here, and often in heroic plays, are parodied in *The Rehearsal* II. iv,
where the usurpers have very little difficulty in defeating the two kings of
Brentford.

Thus godlike, great and good, I should have wished
To have been dethroned before. 'Tis now I live,
And more than reign; now all my joys flow pure,
Unmixed with cares, and undisturbed by conscience.

Enter PALMYRA, AMALTHEA, ARTEMIS,
            DORALICE *and* MELANTHA

LEONIDAS
See, my Palmyra comes! The frighted blood   485
Scarce yet recalled to her pale cheeks,
Like the first streaks of light broke loose from darkness,
And dawning into blushes. – (*to* POLYDAMAS) Sir, you said
Your joys were full. Oh, would you make mine so!
I am but half restored without this blessing.   490

POLYDAMAS
The gods, and my Palmyra, make you happy,
As you make me.

Gives her hand to LEONIDAS

PALMYRA   Now all my prayers are heard:
I may be dutiful, and yet may love.
Virtue, and patience, have at length unravelled
The knots which fortune tied.   495

MELANTHA
Let me die but I'll congratulate his Majesty. How admirably
well his royalty becomes him! Becomes! That is *lui sied*,
but our damned language expresses nothing.

PALAMEDE
How? Does it become him already? 'Twas but just now you
said he was such a *figure* of a man.   500

MELANTHA
True, my dear, when he was a private man he was a *figure*;
but since he is a king, methinks he has assumed another
figure. He looks so *grand*, and so *auguste*. (*going to the
king*)

PALAMEDE
Stay, stay; I'll present you when it is more convenient.
[*aside*] I find I must get her a place at court; and when she 505

497 *becomes* D (Becomes Q1)
500 *figure* ed. (figure Q1)
501 *figure* ed. (figure Q1)
503 *figure* ed. (figure Q1)
     grand (grand Q1)
     auguste (August Q1)

is once there, she can be no longer ridiculous; for she is
young enough, and pretty enough, and fool enough, and
French enough, to bring up a fashion there to be affected.

LEONIDAS (*to* RHODOPHIL)
Did she then lead you to this brave attempt?
(*to* AMALTHEA) To you, fair Amalthea, what I am,   510
And what all these, from me, we jointly owe.
First, therefore, to your great desert, we give
Your brother's life; but keep him under guard
Till our new power be settled. What more grace
He may receive, shall from his future carriage   515
Be given as he deserves.

ARGALEON
I neither now desire nor will deserve it;
My loss is such as cannot be repaired,
And to the wretched life can be no mercy.

LEONIDAS
Then be a prisoner always; thy ill fate   520
And pride will have it so. But since, in this, I cannot,
Instruct me, generous Amalthea, how
A king may serve you.

AMALTHEA   I have all I hope,
And all I now must wish; I see you happy.
Those hours I have to live, which heaven in pity   525
Will make but few, I vow to spend with vestals.
The greatest part in prayers for you; the rest
In mourning my unworthiness.
Press me not farther to explain myself;
'Twill not become me, and may cause you trouble.   530

LEONIDAS (*aside*)
Too well I understand her secret grief,
But dare not seem to know it. – (*to* PALMYRA) Come my fairest,
Beyond my crown I have one joy in store:
To give that crown to her whom I adore.

Exeunt omnes

530 *you* ed. (*your* Q1)

---

515 *carriage* behaviour
526 *vestals* The Vestal Virgins in Rome tended the sacred fire said to have been brought
by Aeneas from Troy. Amalthea is clearly talking about nuns here.

EPILOGUE

Thus have my spouse and I informed the nation,
And led you all the way to reformation:
Not with dull morals, gravely writ, like those
Which men of easy phlegm with care compose,
Your poets of stiff words and limber sense,   5
Born on the confines of indifference;
But by examples drawn, I dare to say,
From most of you who hear and see the play.
There are more Rhodophils in this theatre,
More Palamedes, and some few wives, I fear.   10
But yet too far our poet would not run,
Though 'twas well offered, there was nothing done.
He would not quite the women's frailty bare,
But stripped them to the waist and left them there.
And the men's faults are less severely shown,   15
For he considers that himself is one.
Some stabbing wits, to bloody satire bent,
Would treat both sexes with less compliment:
Would lay the scene at home, of husbands tell

2 *reformation:* ed. (*Reformation.* Q1)
4 *compose,* (*compose.* Q1)
5 *poets* F (*Poet's* Q1)
6 *indifference;* (*indifference.* Q1)
13 *women's* ed. (*Woman's* Q1)

The Epilogue was published, like the Prologue, in *Covent Garden Drolery* (1672), and it was there said to have been spoken by Michael Mohun (1620–?91) who created the part of Rhodophil. Unlike Charles Hart in the Prologue, Mohun here speaks in character, as Rhodophil.

2 *reformation* There is an echo of Prologue 1; and the notion of reformation is taken as lightly there as here.

4 *of easy phlegm* phlegmatic, not passionate, and so easily moral

5 *stiff...sense* Who write without literary ease of moral attitudes they find it easy to recommend. This is a slightly odd line, however, and it is perhaps not too far fetched to suggest that Dryden (and so the actor) might have had in mind that the play just performed, with all its sexual innuendo, was one of stiff sense and limber (that is, easy or pliant) words. The poets here commented on in the Epilogue would then be those whose rigidity of formulation was in stark contrast to the flexibility of their sexual equipment.

6 *indifference* to sexual passion

117

For wenches taking up their wives i'th'Mall   20
And a brisk bout which each of them did want
Made by mistake of mistress and gallant.
Our modest author thought it was enough
To cut you off a sample of the stuff:
He spared my shame, which you I'm sure would not,   25
For you were all for driving on the plot:
You sighed when I came in to break the sport,
And set your teeth when each design fell short.
To wives and servants all good wishes lend,
But the poor cuckold seldom finds a friend.   30
Since therefore court and town will take no pity,
I humbly cast myself upon the city.

---

20 *For...Mell* taking up with prostitutes while unaware that they are in fact their wives. See note at Prologue 20.

25 *shame* of being cuckolded by Palamede

32 *the city* This courtly, lascivious comedy ends with a sneering appeal to the supposedly more upright city for help against the immorality of the audience, which was largely, as we have noted, not from the city. See note at Prologue 24.